Dear Universe, I Get it Now:

LETTERS ON THE ART AND JOURNEY OF BEING BRAVE AND BEING ME

BY A.Y. BERTHIAUME

Be Brave Be You ♥A.Y

ONION RIVER PRESS

Burlington, VT

Onion River Press
191 Bank Street
Burlington, VT 05401
www.onionriverpress.com

Cover Design by Moira Abram-Hale, moiraabram.com

Publisher's Cataloging-in-Publication Data
Names: Berthiaume, A. Y., author.
Title: Dear universe, I get it now : letters on the art and journey of being brave and being me / by A.Y. Berthiaume.
Description: Burlington, VT: Onion River Press, 2020.
Identifiers: LCCN: 2020905287 | ISBN: 978-1-949066-43-2 (pbk.) | 978-1-949066-45-6 (eBook)
Subjects: LCSH Berthiaume, A. Y. | Conduct of life. | Self-actualization (Psychology). | BISAC BIOGRAPHY & AUTOBIOGRAPHY / Personal Memoirs. | SELF-HELP / Personal Growth / General | BODY, MIND & SPIRIT / Inspiration & Personal Growth
Classification: LCC BF637.S4 B4765 2020 | DDC 158/.1/092--dc23

I dedicate this book...

a little bit to:

my grandfathers, Francis and Normand (storytellers and exaggerators),

and my grandmothers, Toni and Georgette (badass and resilient women).

Wherever in the Universe you look down from,
know I am eternally grateful

that both story and strength are in my blood...

and LOTTA-BIT to:

my parents, Leon and Anne,

for walking alongside me on this winding road

and standing with me during the worst of times and the best of them.

You have ALWAYS loved me fiercely.

I GET THAT NOW.

Table of Contents

Disclaimer 1:
PROTECTION OF THE INNOCENT

Names (of characters, organizations, schools, and businesses) within the main body of this work have either been purposefully excluded or changed, with two exceptions:

Sorry, Mom and Dad.

There wasn't really a way around this.

(Let's remember how much we love each other, 'K?)

Names in the Afterword, Acknowledgements, and Fist Bumps for Females sections of this work are included with explicit permission. (Seriously. I have a signed permission slip.)

Disclaimer 2:
DO NO HARM

No animals were harmed in the making of this book.

Some trees were. (Devastating, I know.)

FOR THE PURPOSES OF THIS WORK, i AM DEFINING THE UNIVERSE AS SUCH:

Universe: *(n)* a kind of Higher Power and guiding force, related to and in good company with God (and a serious fan of Jesus), that knows your purpose and what lessons to provide in relation to said purpose, but has no control over the choices you make with what They have presented you along the way; a cosmic force offering you signs and invitations but not interfering with your free will.

(Think of it like They're the CEO and COO of [INSERT YOUR NAME] Inc., and while they call the shots and provide the orders from on high, there's a pretty big distance between Them (the powers-that-be) and little ol' you WAY down here. Ultimately, by the time you receive the message, it's up to you whether you're going to follow Their executive orders or not.

You with me?

Just believe you me, They're going to keep sending you the same damn memos if you ignore them the first time (or second, or third…).

All right. Let's keep going.

Introduction
A NOTE TO MY READER

In kindergarten, we were given a lineless black-and-white composition notebook as a journal where we could practice our letters and writing. I already loved books. Stories. But as soon as I was able to hold a pencil to paper and scribble a poorly written sentence, I felt the power to create my own stories through words. It was thrilling. I became hooked on filling my notebook with my own sentences.

This was when I first felt in my heart that my path, mission, purpose was to be a writer. I was only five. I couldn't explain it or express it. It was a feeling. A knowing. An internal whisper I now recognize as intuition, but one I didn't always listen to or follow even while I have always heard it calling me.

If I were to simplify my childhood into my popular pastimes, they were playing outside in a canopy of trees, making up my own songs and dances; and filling journals with stories, or typing novels on the family computer. My fantasies always included two Ps: Prince Charming and publishing. 'Happily, ever after' was only going to be complete if alongside *love*, was also *writing*.

Thirty years later and I'm finally brave enough to make my own dream come true. I've been on this long and winding journey to arrive at this moment—the moment when I have published a book with my name on it that *isn't* a private journal. This moment when you, my wonderful reader, are consuming this very line.

The cover design pays homage to the beginning of this journey (the black-and-white notebook that began it all). The content of this book honors the journey itself. And the reasons I've chosen letters to the Universe as a device are these:

I've kept a journal nearly my whole life. There have been very few periods where there was no notebook within arm's reach. Most of my journal entries have appeared as letters, as though I am writing *to* someone rather than just exercising my thoughts and feelings about life for my own benefit. They've been more like a dialogue, except I never knew who exactly I was writing to. It just came naturally to write to someone who wasn't me. I recognize now I was writing to a Higher Power.

I've been speaking to the Universe the entire time, trying to filter and sort through life, to understand my experiences, to excavate my layers, to embrace myself and my gifts. And when the visions of this book came to me—and it was, in fact, a vision that came in the early morning hours one spring day in 2019—it appeared as a black-and-white composition notebook with the title: *Dear Universe.*

This book told me what it wanted to be. And I actually listened. An art I've been developing over time.

As such, this book is a whole lot about listening. Listening to ourselves. Listening to our intuition. Listening to the Universe. It's also a whole lot about searching for understanding, being brave as we face our discoveries, and then deciding what to do with them.

There was a time not long ago when I had a ridiculously difficult year. I miscarried my second child, my grandfather passed away, I separated from my husband, moved in with my parents, was with my son (not even two yet) only half of the time, sold our home and filed for divorce. (It was the perfect making for the next hit country music single or a Lifetime movie. Take your pick.)

Standing in the pile of ash that used to be my life, I asked, *How did I get here?* I couldn't see what was ahead through the cloud of *'smogulous'* smoke (to quote the Lorax). An internal part of me knew there was meaning and purpose, but I didn't know what those might be, because life felt so bleak, these events so unnecessary.

I began to do what a lot of us tend to do when all kinds of shit happens all at once. We ask ourselves, "Why?" We look for answers and reasons. We try to determine root causes. We also tend to look for someone to blame. Who played a part? What did or didn't we do to contribute? We try to prevent the same shit from happening again. Even that which is well beyond our control. And while I was asking myself all these questions, I took a long, hard look backward, trying to retrace my steps.

It was a crazy time, attempting to move forward with grit and resilience, while also assessing all that had come before. It was like a puzzle had been put together wrong. My job was to deconstruct it and put it back together right. Except I had no discernible picture on the cover of a box to guide me.

What emerged from this dark moment was a brilliant burst of light. A burst of understanding. A burst of remembering. A burst of discovery. Understanding my journey. Remembering who I had always been. Discovering where I was to go next, and how all my prior experiences wove together to lead me there. What I didn't know as I made this deep soul dive was it would eventually lend itself to this book.

If I have but one hope for you as my reader, it is by listening to my journey, you are inspired to try and understand your own. Or through some relatable or resonating moment I share, you come to understand some part of your own story you had not recognized before. More than that, I hope in reading this, you feel just a little bit braver to be you. Because we all deserve to be just ourselves and to be loved, lifted, seen, and heard for exactly who we are. And that journey starts within us. I get that now.

I've included some reflection questions/journal prompts at the end of each letter to help you along your path. Feel free to stop and think about them as you go, or return to them later. There's also the option to ignore them altogether. There is no right or wrong way to engage with this book. I simply want it to serve you and your own journey.

To learn more about how **Dear Universe** came to be, *go to the Afterword.*

To see other ways you can use this book along your path to bravery, go to **Bravery Boosters: More Stuff for the Reader.**

To start this journey, turn the page.

Letter 1
HOLD YOUR TONGUE

Dear Universe,

You did a great job choosing my parents. They gave me (and my siblings) amazing adages to live by:

If you don't have anything nice to say, don't say anything at all.

All that matters is we're together.

Take initiative.

Don't put all your eggs in one basket.

(I love this one especially, as this was my mother's response when I told her I thought I was in love with a boy in high school and he was 'the one.' For the longest time, I could not figure out what the hell being in love had to do with eggs or baskets. Then, when 'the one' bubble burst, I was so thankful I still had some eggs and a basket left.)

Once you start something, you finish it.

Put yourself in their shoes.

Oh, and my other personal favorite (which was completely my dad's):

Don't call each other a moron.

(This seemed to be our favorite car ride insult. I can still picture the three of us kids thigh-to-thigh in the backseat, my little brother squished unhappily between myself and our big sister, as we head to church.

"Why do I always have to sit in the middle?" my brother whines. His blue-checked, collared shirt is buttoned all the way up, and he tugs at it around his neck.

"You're the youngest and the smallest," my older sister replies, smoothing out her dress on her lap.

"That's not fair," he whines again.

"Don't be such a moron," I say, even though it doesn't make any sense. I pull my plastic head band away from head to release the pressure just above my ears. I don't know what I hate more, the headband or the tights I have to wear. And the back of my head still hurts from where my dad combed straight through a knot in my hair without deliberation or slowing down.

"You're the moron," my brother replies and elbows me.

"You're both morons," my sister jumps in and rolls her eyes.

Via the rearview mirror, Dad gives us the sharp evil eye he inherited from our grandmother. We quiet ourselves. "Don't call each other a moron. I hate that." Then we all try not to laugh.

Here we are decades later, and I keep the word *moron* on the no-fly-list of insults.)

I think You've made children grow up to remember the adages of their parents, either encouraging them to *heed* their parents' warnings or providing incentive to *defy* them, because they weren't useful pieces of wisdom to begin with. There is room for both.

Keep what serves. Discard the rest.

The problem is we don't know how to filter this as kids. What our parents say, for the most part, is what we consider Truth. And, because we are kids, and we're literal beings, we don't understand inference, nuance, metaphor.

I bring this up because, in addition to all those wonderful catch phrases I've got in the memory bank, I also remember these—usually directed *solely* at me:

Hold your tongue.

File your tongue.

Bite your tongue.

Sharpen your tongue.

and

Don't exaggerate.

To me as a kid, these were all variations of PLEASE. STOP. TALKING.

I blame You for this, Universe.

You brought me into this world with a force. A force I didn't know how to wield.

Loud. Opinionated. Communicative. Unabashed. Taking up space. Commanding attention.

Some children can whisper.

I couldn't.

Some children went silent when adults spoke to them.

I didn't.

Some children had only the opinions of the adults around them.

I hadn't.

Some children were inherently more reserved.

I wasn't.

You made me a girl who would walk into the center of the room at a family gathering and demand, hand on hip, everyone quit talking so she could perform "Chantilly Lace." A girl who went to Story Hour at the local library and asserted she be addressed as Dorothy of Kansas (or Oz), since this was the character she was playing that day. (And please don't make her sic the Wicked Witch on you.) A girl who once colored a picture of a barn bright orange, and when asked where all the animals were, replied, "The barn is on fire, and they all ran away." You made me a girl with an arsenal of swift comebacks, witty replies, and too much sarcasm beyond her chronological years to have any sense of appropriate delivery.

No wonder my dad passed out at my birth—he felt the Earth spin on its axis with my *BIGness*. Nurses had to give him my mother's ice chips to settle his stomach once he came-to. Some believe it was the sight of blood (my mom had a c-section); others believe he hadn't eaten anything all day, and his blood sugar was low. I don't really buy either of those.

(I know, I know, *don't exaggerate*).

The point is, I was this little girl with this big booming voice and presence and personality. (I didn't come with an instruction manual, though I'm willing to bet, on more than one occasion, my parents wished they had one. Like all parents do.)

With every plea to hold, sharpen, bite, or file my tongue, I began to hear *don't speak*.

If you do; then censor, refine, or revise what you're saying.

Not to mention, *Please, don't embarrass us.*

Those snappy demands, complete with an ominous tone of voice, or a look from my parents, indicated I was out of line. I had disappointed them (or embarrassed them) with my quick tongue. I hated that. Their approval mattered to me. What they wanted mattered to me. Who they wanted me to be mattered to me—like any child who wants to please their parents.

They may have been constantly trying to reel in my unsolicited comments out of fear of how they themselves would be perceived as parents. Because the actions of our children automatically reflect the actions of us as parents.

There is so much pressure to parent perfectly—whatever 'perfectly' even means. But public judgement is real. The ruthless perception if your child behaves badly it *must* mean that you as the parent are doing X (which is wrong), or aren't doing Y (which is also wrong). I now understand this *as* a parent. It's like a game of how to fail *less,* because you're always caught in a lose-lose.

Do You remember just the other day when I took Kay to the indoor playground? Yeah, the one with the bouncy obstacle course on one side of a big room, and an indoor playground on the other. He didn't want to leave, even though he was totally maxed out.

You'll recall when I told him time was up, he rushed to the play grocery store, grabbed a toy shopping cart (luckily empty) and proceeded to push it toward the playground area, completely ignoring my command. When I calmly walked up to him to speak quietly, to avoid embarrassing him in the common area, he took the shopping cart and shoved it at the playground. I was fuming but tried to remain collected, to avoid hollering at him in public—especially as other parents turned to watch us.

He proceeded to hit me in the face while he screamed, "You're being a giant penis!"

I left the cart where he'd shoved it, picked him up around the waist, and carried him sideways on my hip to the coat room, so his little hands couldn't wail anymore on my cheekbones.

I was partially proud he had used anatomically correct language for his body parts, but also very much horrified he was destroying property and physically assaulting me in front of dozens of other parents with their children. The side-eye from the mother next to me in the coat room, while he continued to tantrum and I struggled to dress him in winter boots and a coat, was enough to let me know she wasn't impressed.

"How could you let him behave like that?" I saw written in the voice bubble above her perfectly brushed hair, as she unbuckled her infant from their car seat.

I wanted to say, "Just wait. Your kiddo will be four someday."

Instead, I said nothing. Not that anyone would have heard a word I said over Kay's carrying on. "You're being unkind!" "You're being mean." And then, outside, as I was trying to get him into his car seat, "Don't hit me!"

In that moment, while I hate to admit it, I thought, "Please stop talking."

But it didn't mean I wanted him to be silent forever or to stop showing up as himself for the rest of eternity. I just needed him to stop talking in that moment. To preserve some dignity in front of Mother of the Year. I realized with a jolt, I needed him to understand what my parents had also wanted me to understand about expressing myself publicly. When I was the child, and my parents were trying to reign me in, it wasn't because they didn't want me to stand in my full force.

What we had was merely an epic failure to communicate.

They said what they needed to say and assumed their messages were being delivered loud and clear with complete understanding. And what I *thought they wanted* from me (to be a little more quiet, a little more contained) mattered to me so much, for the next two-and-a-half decades, I internally struggled to understand who I wanted to be more: the unabashed, unapologetically me at birth, or the tamed and quieter version I assumed my parents preferred.

I get it now.

My parents weren't telling me to hold, sharpen, bite, or file my tongue because they wanted me to shut up and be silent, or because they wanted me to be anyone but myself. What they wanted was for me to learn how to sift and leverage my ability to be vocal. To understand context and audience. To be able to feel the energy of a room and play to a crowd. To think about what I was saying before I just blurted out what was in my head. To understand the costs associated with putting myself out there in BIG ways. To understand the power of my voice and my words.

The ACTUAL lesson has finally been received.

I don't have to stop talking or shut up. And I don't have to be anyone but me.

But it doesn't hurt to *Think about what you're going to say, before you say it.*

That, I must admit, is sound advice from Mom and Dad. So, I'll keep that one.

Sorry for being such a moron this entire time,

The recovering middle child

QUESTIONS FOR YOUR PATH TO BRAVERY

What are some of the rules you were given as a child
you can now discard?

Which can you reframe?

What new ones do you want to create and live by?

Letter 2
TREE HUGGER (AND KISSER)

Dear All-Knowing Universe,

Was I a tree hugger or forest dweller in some earlier life?

I remember looking at trees for hours and hours through car windows. I loved Snow White and the Seven Dwarfs and Sleeping Beauty, with their quaint little cottages in the woods and all their animal friends. My favorite pastime was being outside, barefoot, playing in the canopy of trees next to my parents' or the small woods behind my grandparents' house (who lived next door).

I was called to be out there. I hadn't learned it from anyone. My parents weren't great outdoors people, evident by the one and only failed camping trip. I did have one grandfather and some uncles who hunted, but I wasn't out there with them learning how to load or clean a rifle, track a deer, or shoot to kill. (As a kid, I most certainly could not wrap my head around willingly scenting myself with deer pee. You and the Big Guy must find that voluntary human behavior for the sake of sport pretty hilarious.)

It could be as a native-born Vermonter, my love of trees is somehow innate. A part of the life and landscape I was born into. Whatever it was that connected me to the woods, I found myself there a lot. This was where I performed musicals I loved, or where I created my own.

In that circle of trees next to the garage, there had been a massive pine cut down well before my birth, but the stump remained. For years that stump was a soap box. A stage. A platform.

I would make up extensive plots, and then burst into made-up songs along the storyline, singing them loudly from that stump. I would make up dances to go with my songs. At least once in a number, I would need to jump from that wooden platform in enthusiasm and then do-si-do with a tree. Since most of the trees had slim enough trunks, I could get my arm hooked around them all right. Sometimes the bark scraped the crease of my arm. For the slower songs, the songs about longing and love, it was more like holding on to them with my palm and leaning out, as though they were a lamppost and I a crooner in an old black-and-white picture. Always, no matter the song or the tempo, I would sing as I wove in and around the trees, touching them as I went, pine pitch getting stuck to my fingers and the soles of my feet.

When each song and dance was over, I returned to the plot and dialogue; the trees were stand-ins for characters. I would carry on conversations face-to-face with their raised bark ridges.

"What do you mean you're moving and leaving here for good? Where will you go? I'll come with you."

And then pause for their response.

"I just need one week to get ready. Can't you wait for one week?"

If those conversations were particularly emotional or intimate—I was telling grand stories, you know—there may have been a hug or even a kiss involved. Yes. My first kiss was probably with a pine or a maple. (How many other little girls have made out with trees is my question. Feel free to answer that for me whenever You have a chance. Send Your response by carrier pigeon, if you must.)

For years I pretended, imagined, played in the trees, until one day a cousin saw me speaking with a maple in our grandparents' yard (they lived next door to me) and wouldn't let it go.

"Are you talking to a tree?" he slapped his knee, tossed his head back, and let out a high-pitched squeal. His black t-shirt hung low to his knees. His jeans practically fell off around the waist.

Where had he come from?

I turned my back to him, looked at the grass, and shoved my hands into my pockets. My face was so hot.

Maybe if I just stand still long enough and don't respond...

"Are you fucking crazy?" he asked.

"Jeremiah! Watch your mouth," my grandmother barked from the driveway. "Now, you just leave her be. She's not hurting anyone." She attempted to usher him away with hand signals.

"I want to hear what the tree says back." He laughed harder.

I began to sweat through my clothes.

"You stop that. Now come here." My grandmother pulled him by the arm.

When they both disappeared into the garage, I lifted my head. The tree was now only a tree.

It was the first time I wondered if I had become too old to be playing make-believe. Perhaps my time with the trees should end.

And it did.

I was eleven. Maybe twelve.

After that, I still found myself throwing a blanket onto the grass during summers to read or write on the lawn. Looking at the woods in mine and my grandparents' yards, longing to be a little girl again.

I got the smallest taste of being back in the solace of the woods in the fall, when pre-season for field hockey had us running laps on the cross-country trail.

While there were no woods or trails nearby my undergrad college in Ohio, in grad school I became an avid runner and spent my morning runs on a trail at the metro park. The trail went over little wooden bridges and ran next to streams and around ponds. Secretly, though I was then in my 20s, I imagined all the creatures I came across—the deer, the herons, the rabbits, the birds—were my friends. Some part of me was still Snow White. I still felt such peace, and comfort in the woods.

When all my degrees were earned and I was old enough to have my own living arrangements, my top priority was always to have trees nearby. I was adamant, when my then husband and I bought a house, we find one with a yard and trees. I said it was because I wanted our future children to have the same experience of a yard and outdoor play I had, but really, I wanted it for me, too.

Now, living in a condo in a highly residential area, I have to make peace with the few trees that separate my home from the medical buildings and parking lots that bump up against it. I regret not having a private yard or trees for Kay and his imagination to run rampant in. Every now and then, when I take him to a nearby trail in the woods, I see the same wonder unfurling, the delight, respite, and safety the trees once provided me. And every time he takes his shoes and socks off and asks to run barefoot, I know he is so much a part of my soul and my being that just maybe he *doesn't* need trees. I provide shelter and freedom for him instead. I am his roots.

Still, for me, childhood was infused with the trees that provided a landscape for just being me. They offered me my first stage. My first tribe. We had a pact, and they were a loyal following. They never told me what I had to say (or sing) didn't matter. They stood by me in silence but didn't request silence in return. More importantly, they set the example for who I want to be toward others, and who I want others to be for me—to see me, to hear me, to stand by me in my fullest expression.

Even now I feel like You lead me out to the woods for solace, reflection, comfort. Those trails just around the corner, feeling familiar and safe as soon as I'm immersed in the woods and no longer able to see the parking lot, only little pieces of sky visible between the branches and leaves—it's like being welcomed home.

I guess I'll *leaf* it here,

Forest dweller in an alternate life

QUESTIONS FOR YOUR PATH TO BRAVERY

What brings you solace and comfort?

Who or what gives you space to be true to yourself?

Where and/or when do you feel the freest to be seen and heard as your authentic self without censorship or alteration?

Letter 3
WIELDING A MIGHTY PEN

Hey, Universe,

I'm pretty sure becoming a writer stemmed from one of the earliest instances of sexism I can remember and not entirely because we were required to practice our letters and spelling in our journal every week, which I loved as soon as I could hold my pencil straight. That one group of five and six-year old boys told me I couldn't be a Teenage Mutant Ninja Turtle because I was a girl. And because I was a girl, I needed to be the girl reporter, April O'Neil.

(I'm not sure why You're laughing. This was a serious injustice.)

Though I attempted to make a case for myself, it was useless. They couldn't conceive of rotating who played which turtle and who played April—which would have been a completely fair and compromising solution, in my opinion. They were boys, therefore they were the turtles. I was a girl, therefore I was April. (Or Splinter, the rat, because that was the only other option.)

I mean if this was not sexism and an illustration of how early gender roles and norms are identified, assigned, and carried out, then I want someone to explain to me what it was. Of course, I didn't see it all like that at five. I didn't know the word *sexism*, and sure as shit I wouldn't have known how to spell it, define it, or use it in a sentence.

But looking back, I can see it so clearly.

Boys were heroes. Boys were protectors. Boys were strong and powerful. Boys were in charge. Boys could be ninjas. Boys made the rules. Boys provided ultimatums.

Girls were victims needing to be saved and rescued; they were not the hero or the protector. Girls could be smart and intellectually equipped, but they weren't physically strong or powerful. Girls weren't in charge; they reported to someone else. Girls couldn't be ninjas; they kept house for ninjas. Girls followed the rules. Girls settled for the 'lesser of the two evils' presented as options, because it was better than having no options at all. Girls say "yes" to what they're offered because they're not encouraged to say "no."

So, I settled for playing the reporter, because it was better than playing the rat. I settled for playing April, because playing Ninja Turtles with someone (anyone) was more important than not playing it at all. And, because girls/women are encouraged to make the most out of tough (read: unfair) situations, I made the attempt to embrace the role of April.

Luckily, April and I had a few things in common, which helped. Our names both began with an A. We both wanted to be part of 'the club' and in on the action. I was born in April, so it seemed fitting. More importantly, we both seemed to have it more together than our turtle friends. Plus, there was that love of writing *thang* we shared, and the quest for justice. Though admittedly, both of those were still being developed.

My classmates only wanted to do ninja moves. Terrible moves. Moves not based in any practice of martial arts. It was all flailing arms and ridiculous sounds, like cats in heat. Plus, there was the occasional poked eye when they ninja-moved too close to one another. Their interest in being ninja turtles was all about pretending to beat the snot out of the bad guy. Not that I could blame them, really. Wasn't that also why I wanted to be a ninja turtle? To fight off evil and protect the underdog?

But since that option was not available to me, I needed to find my own important way to contribute to the play. It wasn't hard to see these boys had no concept of storytelling. Not like me—the girl with the stump in the backyard, playing leading lady to some old pines and maples. So, every afternoon when I arrived at Lonnie's house (my daycare provider), I sat at an old red school desk and sketched out my own Turtle stories. These were my first works of fiction.

I tried to make my pages look like comic books—a sequence of boxes with little drawings and voice bubbles. Except the spelling was atrocious, and I couldn't write in complete sentences yet. My illustrations were even worse. The four heroes in a half-shell basically looked like green sausage links stuck together with a head and tied together at the joints with colored lines meant to look like bandanas.

Not that it mattered. My friends couldn't read them any more than I could entirely write them.

What was important was I had developed a plot for the rest of us to use as inspiration for the next day of imaginative play. What was important was I found a subtle way to lead the pack and a quiet way to control our direction, whether they permitted my being a turtle or not. *Take that, Boys.*

And isn't that like the real world—even now, regardless of women's movements and the rights we have won? Women who strive to be in positions of power and leadership are still stuck playing supporting roles to the leading Mr. and making their great ideas seem like someone else's. Women still lead from the sidelines, hoping they will be recognized, while also hoping they won't be caught taking charge of the situation and stepping outside of their lane.

The thing of it is, I didn't realize I was trying to manipulate the situation so I could lead. Not then. I just knew I could contribute something these boys couldn't—storytelling, structure, plot—and it gave me a more important role to play than the one they had delegated. Every day, we would huddle at the beginning of free time, and I set the scene for them to follow.

"Okay, so today, Shredder has snuck into our house while we were sleeping and stole all our stuff," I tell them, sitting on the alphabet carpet, pushing my stupid dress down between my crossed legs so they can't see my panties, and readjusting my forsaken headband to release the pressure from behind my ears.

"When we wake up, you are each going to see one of your weapons is missing…"

"Then we'll go after him and we'll karate chop him—HI-YA!" fake Michelangelo chimes in, causing the other three to start karate-chop motions and hyena calls.

"*After* you put together all the clues to where he's headed," I say.

"How do we know what the clues are?" fake Raphael wants to know.

"I'm about to tell you," I grunt, and I tell them the rest of the story according to my comic.

"Ready?" I ask.

They spring from the carpet, barrel into the 'turtle house,' (the indoor playhouse in the center of the room) and pretend to fall fast asleep. Then they rush through the discovery of the clues and eventually find themselves in an epic ninja battle in the middle of the carpet that eventually gives our teacher cause for concern when one wayward kick nearly tumbles over a chair. When that happens, I realize to some extent my stories and structure only go so far. They still bulldoze through all the key plot points just to get to the part where they beat on the imaginary villain, Shredder.

Eventually we are told we can't play Ninja Turtles in the classroom anymore. Our teacher is worried someone will get hurt. I want to tell her it will likely be one of them (the Turtles), but I don't. We find something else to play: dogs. This works in my favor.

We all believed dogs were boys. All of them. Apparently, there were no female dogs in my hometown. You know what that meant? Those Turtles were now dogs. Crawling around on all fours, panting, barking, wanting to be walked and scratched behind the ears. And me? I got to be the owner. Didn't You know all pet owners were girls?

They didn't want me to be a ninja. They didn't want me stealing any of the action, but without my story, they were just bodies swiping through the air occasionally hitting each other. Truthfully, this didn't change much when we introduced playing dogs to our recess time. They still needed my creative direction to infuse our play with meaning. They still looked to me to inform what we did next. I suppose in some ways while it was my first experience with sexism and confining to gender norms, it was also my first experience with leadership and testing how to break through or live with those barriers.

More importantly, it was the discovery of my own superpower. With each of these moments to create and share a new story, to lead a thrilling escapade, and stop a maniacal villain, my need to write swelled inside me. After the Ninja Turtle comic strips, and the little dog stories I made up on the spot, came more handwritten and illustrated works. There was *On Christmas Morning* (a work of creative nonfiction), *Honey and the Kids* (a work of fiction), *Happy Times on Ice* (also fiction), *Winter* (a book of poems), and a long line of other titles that make up my earliest (and most terribly written) endeavors.

Those boys could have their sword, their bow, their twin sai, and nunchucks. They could continue to develop their imaginary art of ninjutsu. I would go on to develop the very real art of storytelling. My weapon was a mighty pen, and I would learn to wield it.

HI-YA!

April

QUESTIONS FOR YOUR PATH TO BRAVERY

What is a superpower of yours? How did you discover it? How do you wield it now?

If you aren't wielding it, why not?

Letter 4
MY (UNFORTUNATE) FIRST FORAY IN NONFICTION

All right, Mr. Funny 'Man,'

You made me suggestible. Not in the way of hypnosis that leaves you scratching your armpits like a monkey every time you hear the word *banana*, but like show me a great character or story and I want to BE that character and LIVE that story.

I look back on childhood and I realize just how influenced I was by the TV shows and movies I watched. My earliest imaginative play and writing were based on characters I was most drawn to, such as Laura Ingalls and Anne of Green Gables—no surprise, considering their personalities and that they, too, had a passion for the pen.

What stood out to me as a child was they were encouraged to write from the heart, write what they knew. When they did, those stories were better written and more believable than the flamboyant fiction they attempted. Naturally, I wanted to 'write from the heart,' too. (You know what happened next…yeah, hilarious.)

I decided what better experiment than to write about the cul-de-sac I grew up on. Seemed like an awesome idea at eleven years old.

Do You remember how I presented this idea to my parents? Because I don't.

But good on them for:

1) not entirely squashing the idea (though looking back, maybe it would have been for the best), and

2) encouraging me to get permission from my neighbors first.

So, I wrote a permission slip asking for everyone's blessing to be featured in my book and left one in each person's mailbox. There were twelve people living on my street at the time, in addition to my family. Ten people signed and returned their form.

"Remember, Alyssa, you can only write about the ten people who gave you permission," my dad reminded me.

I nodded and took my seat at the family computer. I wrote an eleven-page recount of observations and mundane details about everyone, including my family members. There was no story. No plot. Not even a moral. It was just terrible, terrible writing about *really* boring real-life stuff that somehow seemed relevant to me at eleven. Really boring stuff (completely lacking punctuation) like:

"When we first moved in we added another section of the house—a family room, my room, a bathroom, and a hallway. We've also had a series of leaks in the ceiling. Also we have had a lot of light replacements over the years. There's also been computer problems, a dent in our dishwasher, mice in the cellar…"

Say it with me, "Ugh."

Every chapter was a list of observations. *That neighbor lets us use her pool. This one always says "hi." That one must really love to garden because it's the only thing I ever see her do. Here's why I love my grandparents living next door.*

Then because that wasn't enough, I included a section about the woods where I talked about nearly every single animal I'd given an obvious name, like Mr. Squirrel and Mr. Chipmunk. Then another section about my 'experiences,' which was more a list of injuries I'd sustained (falling off a bike, falling off the bed, etc.) followed by a list of childhood activities I'd mastered, like riding a bike—well, sort of mastered.

This first foray into nonfiction was a disaster. Of course, I couldn't see that right away. I was quite proud of that 'manuscript' when it was finished. I was sure it was just like the stories Laura and Anne would have produced. I'd written about my people, my home. Eleven typed pages felt like a serious accomplishment.

Once it was 'approved' by my parents, my mother helped me print enough copies, hole punch the pages, and put them into green folders with fasteners. This was my idea. The act of binding them into a folder with fasteners was the closest I could get to having them bound like a real book.

I drew a pine tree in colored pencil on the bottom left corner of each cover and hand wrote the title: *Grewing up on the Court*. I returned to the ten people's mailboxes and placed each person's copy inside. Then I waited on the front lawn for people to walk to their mailboxes and pick up their signed copies. I was thrilled.

Many years later, I was not so thrilled.

Not a single person told me about the misspelling in the title. I discovered it myself after years had passed

Why did no one say a thing? I'm guessing because they thought my book was cute. No one was going to tell me it was horrible, because they knew I had worked hard. People weren't going to tell me if what I said was rude, or wrong, or boring, or simply a terrible work of nonfiction. They were going to let me have my moment and not bruise my pride. Bless their hearts. (You probably gave them extra points towards getting into the Good Place.)

Insult to injury (for me, not them), many of them kept their copy FOR YEARS. They didn't trash it. They didn't recycle it. They didn't use it for a bonfire one summer. In my adulthood, the neighbor with the pool told me she still had it. One of the porch-sitting old ladies still had possession of it when she passed on. I got my grandparents' copy back after they passed away—my parents found it tucked in on their bookshelf (probably wedged between actual literary masters). The neighbor girls I used to play with—their mom was the woman with the pool—told me only recently, they're pretty sure she *still* has her copy.

While it's been mortifying to me to know my earliest (and most embarrassing) work of nonfiction is still around in quantity twenty-four years later, it has also been intriguing. Intriguing as to why all these people have kept this little folder with some of my earliest thoughts.

For them, did they keep it because they were truly touched to have been featured, regardless of what was said? Were they delighted to be noticed? To be cared for and recognized enough to have someone *want* to write about them…for someone to have something to say about them, even if that someone was just a child?

It is so powerful and meaningful to be seen and heard. It makes one feel less alone; like they belong. And isn't belonging so very important? Isn't it satisfying to be recognized?

For me, this book stands out because it was the first time I tried to give voice to others on the page. It was my attempt to capture them, their essence. To bring them to life. To memorialize people in sentences. These were very poor attempts, but attempts, nonetheless. Anything we do starts with the very first try.

I've been given a gift to see beyond peoples' surface and to capture the deeper parts within. This book, this first book with the terrible misspelling and terrible writing, may have been my attempt at uncovering the gift I did not yet know I possessed. So be it that I went for it, inspired by Laura or Anne, my imaginary, TV-based friends. It was a purposeful first experiment.

Am I getting this right, Universe? Is that what my first work of nonfiction—kept by way too many—is all about?

Growing to understand more and more all the time,

Current member of Obsessive Spell-Checker Anonymous

QUESTIONS FOR YOUR PATH TO BRAVERY

What's something you remember trying for the first time you "failed" at (or didn't go perfectly)?

What did you learn from it at the time? What can you learn from it now?

What inspired or motivated you to try it to begin with?

Letter 5
CONFRONTATIONALLY CHALLENGED (AND WHITE)

So, Universe,

Can we get real, here?

I hate tough conversations. I hate confronting my feelings with other people who may have hurt them or talking about the needs I need met. I also hate trying to speak about something I feel passionately about to an audience of people who are all grumbly and thinking, "Please stop talking," and/or who are closed off to hearing anything other than their own argument.

I feel like this is one of Your little inside jokes about me specifically. I envision You and God talking about me being all like, "Let's make her loud, bold and opinionated, but *really terribly awkward* at actually talking about the hard stuff."

Thanks, a lot.

When it comes to having tough conversations, the ones I know are going to make the other party uncomfortable or will hurt their feelings, I get an F+. I try to neutralize. Empathize. Understand where the other person is coming from. When I'm done doing all that mental work to try to understand the situation, I talk myself out of approaching the conversation altogether. I *shelve* those arguments or dialogues, as my therapist once told me.

"You put that topic in a box and stick it way up on a shelf, telling yourself you'll bring it down later, when the dust has settled and everyone can talk about it clearly. Except you never actually bring it back down."

I nodded as she said this to me, envisioning myself placing the step stool ever so quietly on the linoleum so no one could hear me. Then stepping barefoot onto the top step and slowly, carefully pushing a shoe box up over the kitchen cabinets. Right next to it is a long line of other shoe boxes. *Hey, wait a minute, how did all those other ones get up there?*

Simply put, I knew she was right.

Except there are some things that *can't* be shelved. Some things that *can't* be ignored. Some things where you must speak. I want to live in the grey place (that neutral zone between opposing forces), where I am able to reason and empathize and see all the sides and angles. Except the grey zone often means just being in the middle, not making a hard decision, or taking a stance. Rarely can you *actually* function from the middle. An authentic life, a deeply rich and meaningful life, can't be lived in that middle place where, oftentimes, complacency is fostered. Being walked over can occur. And silence can be further cultivated.

A beautiful world and human race can't be created out of inaction, or stagnation, or silence, either. Which means there will be times we must choose the step we take, the path we walk, and how we show up for the life and world we want. The current version of myself believes I must be brave in showing up as myself in my own life as much as being brave to show up for the world. What I do personally does extend globally.

The first time I learned this, I learned it the hard way. I was in the sixth grade and it was the first time I had ever heard the 'n' word used outside of TV or books. The first time I had a friend of color. The first time I considered whether my town was racist. The first time I grappled with understanding that saying nothing is the same as doing nothing.

And doing nothing was as harmful as the words that *were* spoken.

I was twelve when Nadia moved to town. Nadia was black. She brought the number of nonwhite students in elementary school to five. She was moving to the area because her mother (a pastor) was going to lead a local church. That local church happened to be the one Lonnie attended [my daycare provider, remember], and so when the family moved here, Lonnie asked if I would take Nadia under my wing and help her meet kids at school.

I WAS PUMPED!

I longed to know of other people and places outside our small town, 'Whitesville.' Meaning, had she been Latina or Indian or Chinese, I would have been equally as excited. When my family decided to host a foreign exchange student from Indonesia for a year, I was every bit as excited. People who *weren't* just like me (white, Catholic) were exciting for me, because they were a glimpse into the greater, bigger, more fascinating world beyond state lines. The immense, big, beautiful world, full of *all* its wonderful people and places beyond Vermont, thrilled me.

My only education about race up to that point was either what I was exposed to on TV (*The Fresh Prince of Bel-Air; Hanging with Mr. Cooper; Family Matters*); or what I read in school (*To Kill a Mockingbird; Roll of Thunder, Hear My Cry*); or what we studied in history (the Civil War; Martin Luther King, Jr.). Notice, too, "race" in these instances meant African American, and that was it. As though there were only white people and black people. And forget "ethnicity." That was hardly even discussed. It was as though race and ethnicity were the same.

Nadia was a real person—not a TV or book character. She had tangible experiences and stories. I wanted to know everything from her actual, real-life perspective. Yes, I probably did come across like wanting to observe a rare specimen. But at the time, being uneducated in diversity, living in a mostly rural place in the early 90s, she was that.

It wasn't long after we were introduced we started spending loads of time together. I asked her questions I wouldn't have asked—or wouldn't have needed to ask—of my white friends. She asked me what she previously hadn't needed to ask her friends either, never having lived in such a predominantly white community.

We talked about our hair. We talked about our skin. I learned about hair extensions and what the words *nappy* and *ashy* meant. We talked about the 'n' word and the difference between the -*a* or the -*er* at the end. I learned about its appropriate social etiquette within the black community—which I had always thought was as simple as: NEVER by any means USE this word!

She asked about country music, assuming that's what all white people liked. We talked about what young girls talk about, too. Boys. Celebrities. TV shows. Music.

While we were fascinated with each other and enjoyed the space to ask whatever we were thinking, truthfully, there was not a lot we had in common. The celebrities, TV shows, and music we liked were different. I wanted to read books, and write stories, and do crafts. I was not one of the 'cool kids' at twelve, and I didn't have any deep interest in boys yet. Nadia preferred reading magazines that were up on the celebrity gossip, and taking the quizzes (about the type of kisser you

32

are and that sort of totally-useless-but-eat-it-all-up-because-it's-'cool' material), getting her nails done, wearing makeup, and engaging in never-ending amounts of 'boy talk.'

Regardless of what we didn't have in common, she was new, I liked her, and I didn't want her to be left out. I tried to draw her into my pre-established group of friends. There were other girls who were boy-crazy and already wearing makeup. Even if I couldn't talk about any of Nadia's interests with either knowledge or enthusiasm, someone else could.

It didn't quite work out like that.

Nadia was bold and confident and not really interested in being part of a petty girls' group. There was no denying even the girls I considered friends erred on the side of creating drama or competition with one another. Especially as far as boys were concerned. So, if Nadia *appeared* to be overtly flirting with a boy one of the girls had 'ownership of,' that was a problem.

She already attracted a lot of attention, not necessarily because she was black (though that was obviously part of it, being in such a white landscape), but because she was tall, curvaceous, voluptuous. She could have passed for eighteen already, while the rest of us still had our child bodies—straight, flat, lanky. The boys were just coming into puberty, and they got all screechy-voiced and red in the face when a girl they thought was 'hot' talked to them. Nadia turned their faces shades of red we had never seen before.

Neither my friends nor I had that effect on those faces. It wasn't an issue for me, but I can't say the same for the others.

Tension was a constant in my girl group and I was always in a mediation among them. If I sided too much with Nadia, it was like I was disowning my original pack. If I sided too much with my group,

I was small-minded and not willing to take a stand. It was *us* versus *them*, and I was trying to be neutral, on neither side. I wanted to be diplomatic. You know, stay in the grey zone where it was comfortable. It occurs to me now the strains were a consequence of all the deeply woven bias, stereotypes, or ideas that underlay my classmates' and friends' attitudes toward anything Nadia did.

Except at the time, I was certain it was elementary-school cattiness: girls with a lack of self-esteem and sense of worth. It just wasn't in my lexicon to consider it may have been a race issue. And I wouldn't come to understand *intersectionality* until grad school, so it didn't occur to me it could be three issues stacking on top of each other—age, gender, *and* race. I just wanted everyone to give each other a chance. I thought that was simple enough.

That wasn't about to happen.

One afternoon in early spring, we walked from one side of the playground to the other, in a clump. We all felt too old to be on the swing sets and it was either too muddy or still too wet with snow to pick a spot to sit and hang. The basketball courts and soccer fields were swarming with boys, peeling off their coats as they worked up a sweat. From one side to the other, we walked and talked as we went. I was at the front, and Nadia was in the back. I couldn't hear what the girls three rows back were talking about, so I have no idea what began the argument between Nadia and another girl, Jenny, but I wouldn't be surprised if it had to do with a boy; all of their previous arguments had to do with boys.

As voices rose, girls behind me stopped walking and turned to watch. Nadia jutted out a hip and crossed her arms. She had a fierce look on her face. Before I could figure out what was what, Jenny called Nadia the 'n' word.

I whipped around to deliver a scathing reply, knowing enough about overt racism, at least, to know that was *never acceptable*, but I was stunned, and tongue tied. Nadia came barreling through the group with her full body, running her shoulder hard into me as she passed.

"These are the people you want to hang around with?" she growled and then stormed off for the doors. No one from my group followed her.

I turned to Jenny and everyone stared at me.

"How would you like it if someone called you a white trash bitch?" I snarled at her.

I still don't know where those words, or my voice, or even that idea came from. I was striving for the white-person equivalent to the 'n' word, but I couldn't come up with any words harsh enough. I just knew I wanted to hit her as hard as I could without actually hitting her. It worked, even though I didn't feel it did justice.

Jenny's eyes welled up. She turned and walked in the opposite direction. A handful of girls went with her.

"Don't you think that was a little harsh?" one of the other girls asked me.

"Harsher than the 'n' word?" I snapped, in total disbelief at this question.

The rest of the group dispersed.

When the bell rang to signal recess was over, I looked for Nadia in the halls, hoping to catch her on her way back to her classroom, but she was nowhere to be found. Then, about a half-hour before school ended, the school's guidance counselor came into my classroom and pulled me out of class. She brought me into the common area just outside all the fifth-grade classrooms and asked me to take a seat. She regaled me with a confusing tale.

Nadia had come to her and told her about the playground. But in her tale, I was a culprit and conspirator instead of a champion. Jenny had also gone to a teacher who went to the counselor, and in Jenny's version, I called her what I had, but she left out the part about her own use of the 'n' word.

I was being charged with all counts.

"Would you like to tell me, in your words, what happened?"

I provided my side of the story, including the rising tension among the group. I didn't deny my own name calling, but I wanted to set the record straight. I was attempting to teach Jenny a lesson and defend Nadia, all at the same time.

"I see," the counselor said nodding, but she still looked so disappointed in me. There was this pause before she spoke again.

"You know, people see you as a leader."

"They do?" My eyes were filled with tears, even though I didn't know why I was crying.

"You have a powerful voice. So, when you speak, others will listen and follow. And sometimes, even when you don't."

I wiped the tears from my eyes.

"I'm going to have to talk to both Nadia's and Jenny's parents."

And then I went hot with anger. I inferred she meant she was going to tell Nadia's parents how I didn't do more, but somehow *let* this happen. She would tell Jenny's parents I called her terrible names. Instead of being the mediator and peacekeeper, I was the bad guy. Because I hadn't picked a side firmly enough? Because I hadn't used my voice well enough? Or early enough? Had my not saying anything sooner been the same as though I, too, called Nadia the word that should never be uttered?

That afternoon, as I arrived at Lonnie's, she asked me what happened. She had received a call from her pastor. This time I sobbed through the whole recount. She believed I had done the best I knew how and was frustrated the school had placed so much responsibility on my shoulders. But she also spoke to me about my use of name calling as a way to face down adversity.

"You can't fight hate with hate," she said. "And you also need to know some of your friends don't like her because she's black, and sometimes we are guilty by association. Except they may not tell you that's why they don't like her, and they may not even know it themselves."

I was so confused. I wanted Nadia to have friends and to feel included. I also wanted to have friends and feel included. *What should I do?* I wondered.

Jenny didn't speak to me for months, so no apologies were made immediately even though for a long time I didn't feel she really deserved one.

Nadia never spoke to me again, so any attempts I made to call her and apologize or make amends were not received.

I was twelve, and I did the best I could with what I knew and thought—which was narrow, clearly. As someone who went on to learn more about racism and white privilege, to want to understand my place in the world in all its colors, I wish I had known more *then*.

I realize now I never could have understood just how sharp a cut the 'n' word was for Nadia to hear. I could never have understood her reality—being one of only five students of color in an entire school, an entire community. How isolating that must have been. How challenging. How infuriating and maybe even, impossible to deal with. I wasn't in touch with my whiteness; I hadn't any reason to be. I wanted so desperately for everyone to just treat each other equally, to see each other equally, to not see difference, that I didn't address it or refused to see it—until it came to that moment, when it was too late.

There are some instances where standing in the middle just doesn't cut it. A side must be chosen. Speaking and using my voice will be required. If, and when, I don't get it quite right, I have to be open to being corrected. If, and when, I piss other people off, because their feelings are hurt or their own participation in something is questioned, I have to be ready to have the tough conversation. Because ignoring something doesn't mean it doesn't exist or it goes away.

Fighting fire with fire also doesn't put out the flame. Ultimately, if I want to live an authentic life in a richly diverse and beautiful world big enough for all of us, I'd better speak up, stand up, and do something about it. Confrontationally challenged or not, I must continue to practice using my voice, and cultivate the power it has in helping me achieve my needs and the needs of others. I'll always be white, but I'll always strive for *not* being silent, even when shit gets real, life gets hard, and words seem to fail.

With commitment to a better life and world,

Still a confrontationally challenged (and white) person

QUESTIONS FOR YOUR PATH TO BRAVERY

When have you felt conflicted showing up for someone else or standing up for a cause you believe in?

How can you do better the next time? How can you reconcile it now?

Letter 6
TICKING TIME BOMB

Dear Dr. U.

I am in recovery for Accomplishment-Identity (also known as Overachiever Syndrome). Would You ever be able to tell me how many others suffer from this? I know it's not in the DSM-5, but at the very least it should be listed among the symptoms of Anxiety Disorder.

I would describe a person with Accomplishment-Identity (AI) as someone who attaches their sense of self, and self-worth, to the number of goals they achieve, groups they participate in, credentials they obtain, etc. When they achieve one goal, they reset the to-do list. They never get any actual joy from what they just achieved, because they've already moved on to the next item on the list. Attached to the achievement is the need for external recognition, which validates the most recent accomplishment, but only temporarily—like a small hit of adrenaline to the self-esteem, only it wanes. Along with this marching along from one item to the next is a distaste for others who are not reliable, or who impede the progress toward an achievement. As such, the person with AI bulldozes through others to get the job done.

Yes, I've given this a lot of thought.

I've been suffering from this since I was ten, when a teacher wrote on a report card in the Areas Needing Improvement Section: "taking on too much and stretching herself too far." I was in the fourth grade and already doing too many things. No wonder, then, by the time I was just on the other side of middle school, I was given a nickname even now, in my 30s, I worry about. I'm terrified I'll slip back into the behavior of the girl who once earned this name: Ticking Time Bomb. A girl who was so maxed out, so out of alignment, she used to erupt. Here's that story:

I walked past the front desk and glanced at the clock above it. There were only ten minutes left before the bell would ring for first period. My bookbag was heavy on my shoulder, full of my textbooks, and I loathed that this day would begin with College Prep Bio.

Gross.

A girlfriend walked toward me, glancing behind her every couple of paces. Her hair was parted down the middle, with pig tails laying down either shoulder. She wore her field hockey jersey.

"Hey," she said casually, but I could tell by the way she surveyed the space around her she didn't want to be overheard.

"What's up?"

"Well. I don't want your feelings to be hurt, but I don't want you to hear it from someone else…"

Great. Some *other* rumor. They weren't foreign to me. Earlier that year, a rumor spread that I "went all the way" with my boyfriend over the summer. I was later convinced by trustworthy girlfriends the rumor was started *by* him.

"So, I guess some of the guys in our class have given you a nick name," she said, one eye and eyebrow lifted, and her head cocked to the side.

"Which would be?" I sighed and rolled my eyes.

41

"Ticking Time Bomb."

In that moment, fits of laughter echoed into the high ceiling in the Commons just beyond her shoulder.

"One of those idiots, I'm guessing?" I asked, nodding in the direction of the congregation of boys from our class who were sitting on the top of the lunch tables, feet on the benches, their bookbags tossed on the floor carelessly.

She nodded. "Bart."

Bart was a boy I had "dated" in the seventh grade—if you can call thirteen-year-olds holding hands in the halls and occasionally talking on the phone dating. He was also among the original Ninja Turtles all those years before.

As far as I could tell, I hadn't done anything to him personally to deserve the name. We had never had any issues or contention. In fact, there were very few personal interactions between us anymore. We each had our own friends and activities which, only occasionally overlapped.

"Thanks for letting me know. Guess I'll go have a chat with him."

She nodded and then walked off, quick-paced, toward class, not sticking around to watch. I imagined she didn't want to be found out as the person who told me.

I stormed over to Bart in front of his friends.

By the shade of red his face turned, he certainly didn't anticipate my confronting him. Then or probably ever. And I was brash enough to think I could call him out and this would be the end of it.

"You want to tell me why you've given me a little nickname?" I crossed my arms.

The color of his face deepened further. While his laugh was loud and delightful—drink worthy, really—he was not a center-of-attention, boastful, or extroverted type. Having known him since kindergarten, I knew he was happy to be lost in a crowd and only ever stood out on the soccer field or the basketball court.

While emojis weren't yet a thing, the only way to describe the look on all his friends' faces just then was the grimacing emoji. That 1/3-anxious, 1/3-terrified, 1/3-delighted expression.

He had a choice between answering me honestly in front of them, which would make him "the man of the hour," or lying and denying he ever gave me such a name, which probably would have made him a "wuss" the rest of the day.

I crossed my arms and waited, looking him straight in the eye. He cast his eyes downward and drew a hand up to the back of his neck and rubbed.

"Well…You go a little crazy sometimes…," he started to say, loud enough for his friends to hear. He wiped the palms of his hands on his jeans.

Then they started to disperse, trying to beat the bell for first period, leaving us there staring at each other. With his friends now gone, his voice softened, and this next part he said less like I was the butt of their jokes, and more like a person he wanted to hand a clue.

"…Like, without warning, you just go off. You'll be totally cool, and then suddenly, you're just yelling."

Damn it.

I expected reasons totally unwarranted. Reasons that were unjustified, that I could refute.

"You're an asshole," I said, and turned before I dared let him see me cry.

I had desperately wanted the nickname to lack merit. I had confronted him assuming it would be. But he wasn't wrong. I knew it as soon as he said it. Moments immediately came to mind that were illustrative of the very behavior he was calling me out for. What made the nickname hurtful wasn't *who* said it, or that it was *being* said, but that it was true, and I couldn't deny it.

As the class president, I was often in charge of student body activities, and when the whole group wouldn't just do what they needed to, I would lose my mind. Yelling. Barking orders. Name calling, even.

"Stop being a bunch of idiots and just do *x, y, z* already."

I did this at rehearsals for the skit competition when people weren't listening. I did this at school spirit assemblies when I had to rally classmates to participate, frustrated that people didn't just volunteer. I did this at student council meetings when we spent more time goofing off than getting anything done. I probably did it at National Honor Society and yearbook meetings, or even musical rehearsal and Field Hockey practices.

No matter the circumstance, I'd often show up starting from a place of humor and being the life of the party, because that was the part of the me people liked. The extremely sarcastic, witty part of me that made people laugh. Then, as we wasted a lot more time and got very little actually done, I would snap. The life-of-the-party buzz wearing off, and the get-down-to-business-beast rearing its head. From one extreme to another, and no one could see it coming.

I had no balance between having fun and getting the job done. One half of me wanted to belong and lead the party, and the other half of me wanted to move and shake and get shit done. Even then, "done" wasn't good enough. I wanted it done with precision and perfection.

I had been given a nickname I deserved. How many had witnessed me lose my cool and were calling me "ticking time bomb" behind my back? How was I going to lead my class when they were all just waiting for me to blow up?

(It occurs to me now, Dr. Universe, this episode strangely echoes that guidance counselor telling me I was seen as a leader, and if I speak, people listen and follow. Except in this instance, I was apparently speaking, and people didn't like what they were hearing... Yes, I'm aware it's about the delivery not the message. Thank You.)

I became paranoid about how many people likened me to a bomb or volcano. I thought the best way forward was to swallow it all down. Pretend the nickname didn't exist. Do my best to *never* allow myself to be seen exploding again—suppress every desire to tell them all to "shut up and get to work." The very fact I had confronted my classmate about the name in the first place was exactly the behavior they would be looking for to support their conclusion. I needed to reign myself in. That family motto, "bite your tongue," whispered inside my ear.

I needed to change. I needed to get rid of this nickname. I needed to be the person they all wanted me to be. I also still needed to accomplish, accomplish, accomplish, but I had to find a different way when it came to motivating a group to perform. There had to be a different way to lead.

Being called Ticking Time Bomb was the first time a peer had held a mirror up to my behavior and said "Look." That was the moment I knew I needed to start paying more attention to myself. To figure out how much was them (just not being cooperative), and how much was me (not being communicative). I became curious about myself and my behavior, but also confused. The debate between being myself or changing myself was forged, and it was all messy and mixed with questions about leadership. Why did I choose to run for Class President? Or, if I was given such a powerful voice, one to lead, how did I use it? Who was I doing any of this for? Who did I want to be, and was that for me or for someone else?

In high school, my over-involvement was partially because I was interested in the new opportunities. I wanted to learn this or that. I wanted to explore new interests. Having new experiences was important to me. The other half, however, was that *I knew* how impressive all my activities would look on my college application. The college application would be *proof* of how well-rounded, motivated, dedicated, and *accomplished* I was. At least that's what I thought.

I carried this mentality into college, this time setting my goal to get into a Ph.D. program. I did the same thing I did in high school and threw myself into extra curriculars, some of them with leadership roles. My schedule was filled with club meetings and practices, and while semesters would start off high-energy and enthusiastic, I would eventually burn out and fall into the same exhausted, unhappy heap I always seemed to find myself in.

I tacked on new roles or activities with the excitement of having a new experience and opportunity, but with no regard to how I would get it all done, how badly it might burn me out. I grew to resent every activity, as I was sapped of energy, or clarity, or breath. How did that translate, then, to the groups I was in, and especially those that I led?

Well, it turned out no differently in college than it had in high school. Coming together, and then not achieving anything, wasn't acceptable to me. I didn't have time to waste. Which meant I lost my shit on people (in the worst-case scenarios), because I was maxed out and right back to wondering why I had joined in the first place.

It's all so clear to me *now*.

Since college, I've tempered the wild AI beast so that it doesn't roar at people as a form of leadership or achieving our goals. Yet, I still have to watch out for it. I now know that when my patience with a group thins, it is quite possible I've found myself in the wrong group of people—people I'm not aligned with—or that I'm no longer aligned with the mission of the group. I've served my time, and it's now time to move on.

I also must watch my own level of mounting excitement when a new opportunity—a class, workshop, conference, event, farmer's market, play, festival—arises. I'm so enthusiastic about what life has to offer, so aware that we only get to live once, that I want to revel in all the splendor. Except now I know how it all ends when I say YES to everything and NO to nothing, all for a feeling of accomplishment that only lasts so long.

I aim to make more careful choices. To be intentional in asking myself, "Does this [insert thing] serve me right now?" To honestly look at my schedule and get real with myself. Most importantly, I try to remind myself that, whether I go and participate in that new activity/venture/opportunity or not—whether I get involved or I don't—I'm *not less than* because I didn't or because I said no.

Even knowing all of that, I struggle with deciding when to adapt to and accommodate a group, and when to say "no." Honoring my own feelings, showing up exactly as I am, and not needing the approval of the group or its individual members. The balance between self and others is a delicate line.

When the people around you view you as a leader, or the person in charge—the person they can rely on for direction, guidance, support—it's like there is no room for error. To show up as yourself, while everyone watches to see what you do, is scary. You feel like they are waiting for you to screw up. You're up on a pedestal, and anyone up that high is likely to fall at least once, even if you're not barking orders and screaming the whole way down.

Understanding my Accomplishment-Identity issue has been a life-long uncovering. (I'm on the 12,000-step program to recovery.) My doing, and doing more, and forever striving for the next item/task/goal, has always been linked to my sense of self-worth. Sure, I've looked confident to everyone around me, but that wasn't the truth most of the time.

What I can say is, along with the challenges AI has created, it has also been incredibly useful. I can work a to-do list like nobody's business, prioritize like a champ, and get shit done efficiently. I'm an organizational ninja (FINALLY. A NINJA!) and a project management master. In both my busy professional and personal lives, these are amazingly useful qualities to have. It's just that they aren't as important as rest, reset, celebration, boundaries, and a self-esteem that is attached to *who I am,* rather than what I achieve.

Now when I start to slip into old habits and patterns…when I start to feel out of alignment…I hear that *tick tick tick,* and I remember it's time to cut the wires, hit the pause button, quit worrying about the clock, and back away from the 15 to-do lists.

Checking off the list that I wrote to You,

Your overachieving to-do list ninja

QUESTIONS FOR YOUR PATH TO BRAVERY

What is a true element of your personality or behavior, but is
hard to face?

How does it serve you? How does it hurt you?

Letter 7
WHEN THERE ARE NO WORDS

Oh, Universe, You Complicated All-Knowing Being,

For as long as I can remember, I've believed you bring people into our life for a reason. They each offer us something we need—be it good, or bad, or hard, the lesson is necessary. The lessons they deliver will eventually be used somewhere else along the way. Without a doubt, Sophia was one of the people you offered me on this journey.

I met Sophia in 2000. I was fifteen and a freshman in high school.

It was fall and those of us interested in joining an Adopt-a-Grandparent program were offered a bus ride to visit the local assisted living center. This program was designed to match students with residents. For those of us who were new to Adopt-a-Grandparent, that was the day we were to be paired off with our 'grandparent.'

When the bus arrived, we were ushered into the activities room in the lower level of the center and introduced to the Activities Coordinator, Betsy. She ran through the requirements of being a volunteer for this program and then started to review profiles of the elderly participants, giving us their name, a few personality traits, and activities they liked. From there it was a free-for-all, students calling out "I'll take him!" or "I'll take her!" as though the residents were being auctioned and our hands were the paddles, what we could 'pay' based on the vigorousness of our waves or how high we stretched our fingers to the ceiling. I found it odd to jump in and claim someone on such a short description.

"Now, we have one participant, Sophia, who is very sweet and could really use company, but she'll be challenging to visit. Her disease has progressed, so she cannot speak."

Crickets.

There was my answer. No one else wanted her.

I raised my hand. "I'll take her," I heard myself say. (I wanted to smack myself for becoming a parrot.)

"Oh, terrific. Let me speak with you privately, once we get everyone situated, OK?" Betsy asked, then quickly moved on to the rest of the matchmaking.

So, I waited for everyone to get paired and begin to disperse to their grandparents' rooms. I held back. Betsy turned to me when the room was clear.

"I just wanted to give you some background on Sophia, because she's one of our more difficult cases and I want you to be prepared."

I was given the rundown.

Sophia had early onset Parkinson's. The only reference I had for her disease was a grandaunt who tremored so badly, I could get motion sickness just watching the back of her head during Sunday morning mass. Sophia's Parkinson's was far worse—not to diminish what my beautiful grandaunt experienced.

Sophia was confined to her wheelchair. She'd lost all faculties of her body, including her ability to speak. The remaining movement she had was in her neck and in her hands—neither of which were fast nor strong. Her remaining ability to use her hands meant she could communicate using a small computer to type her replies—but it took her a while. Her brain remained sharp, and her eye contact fierce. However, it was only a matter of time before even her hand movement declined. She had family nearby, but was visited infrequently.

A perfectly intact mind trapped in a non-working body. No ability to speak. Family, but no visitors. There were no words to describe the horror of this fate. I tried to stifle my heartbreak and focus on what Betsy was telling me.

(Seriously, Universe. Why should anything like that happen to anyone? This was definitely the first time You and the Man Upstairs were on my "bones to pick" list.)

When Betsy was finished, I was taken to the porch—a four-season room with lots of windows, situated at the end of a hall. The porch was right next to Sophia's room, which was convenient, and it had a big TV with a nice sitting area. It was cheerful. The walls were canary yellow and the curtains white and flowy.

My heart pounded inside my ears with each step. What do you say to a person who can't speak back? Suddenly I feared I wasn't up to the task. What could I offer her? How would this work?

Betsy went in ahead of me and bent over to speak to Sophia, who was sitting in her chair facing the TV, her head dipped low and to the left. Apart from a grey-haired and frail body slumped in a wheelchair, I had yet to make out her face, with Betsy standing between us.

As Betsy stepped aside, I could see Sophia turning her head to look at me, slow and labored. I stepped in front of her and got down on my knees so she wouldn't have to strain, and I looked at her.

She had these round, blue eyes that still showed such life. Her eyes devastated me. And while she couldn't move her mouth into a smile, the corners of her eyes crinkled. They shone with a light from inside her, reminding me of that moment when the Grinch's heart grew three sizes too big.

I cleared my throat and willed my voice not to shake.

"Hi, Sophia. I'm Alyssa."

Slowly, she pointed at the computer resting on top of the TV. Betsy passed it to her and then bent back down to eye level.

"Sophia, I'm going to leave you two to visit."

A quick blink of Sophia's eyes confirmed she understood. Blinking was the only motor movement she could still control. The smallest bit of mercy on this woman.

Alone with me, Sophia took to her keyboard and began to type a message, one drawn out letter at a time:

"It's nice to meet you."

While our first thirty minutes together seemed painfully long— each exchange of dialogue taking a dozen times longer than a normal conversation—I never let my attention wander. I worried that even the slightest look out the window while waiting for her to type her message might seem like I was bored, annoyed, impatient, or would give her the impression I didn't want to be there.

So, I watched her fingers—how she typed, or if she pointed. I watched her eyes. I watched the drool pool in the corner of her mouth and slowly fall and hang there. And while I found it all so incredibly sad to take her all in as she was, I knew I would be back. Again. And again. I felt she needed me. Or if not me, someone. Someone to know she was still alive.

Over the next couple of visits, I learned her affinity for playing

Legends of Zelda. This was how she passed her hours on the porch, while others gathered to socialize or play other games she couldn't participate in. For most of my visits, I found her out there, still navigating the controllers with the limited range of motion her fingers could afford. Being Zelda must have been such a precious gift—a way to live inside an able-bodied character still capable of adventure. A mental escape from being prisoner to her disease. As soon as I would arrive, she'd put the controller in her lap and point to her keyboard.

Over time, we developed other activities, like reading. Her hearing and her eyesight were fine. I could read and she could follow. Sometimes we watched the afternoon soaps. By the end of the first year, I started wheeling her out into the living room to mingle with the other residents, with me as the social buffer and interpreter. Much of the time, I just talked. She would interject with a question or two on her keyboard.

And through our activities, we strengthened our trust. I became comfortable wiping the drool from her face. I liked to imagine she was grateful for that small kindness. That there was more dignity restored in having it wiped away, rather than letting it hang, waiting for it to drop onto her shirt. I began to give her hugs when I arrived, and a kiss on the cheek when I left. And I developed the acute ability to understand, just with the rise and dip of her eyes and eyebrows, if she was excited to see me...or if she was sad to see me go.

By the time I was a senior in high school, three changes occurred.

One, a good friend of mine, Maggie, decided to join the program and tag-team with me visiting Sophia.

Two, Sophia lost the movement in her neck and in her hands. During our visits, Maggie and I held conversations together and Sophia listened. We occasionally roped her in with "yes" or "no" questions.

Two blinks for "yes" and one for "no." I could tell she was still happy when we arrived, and having Maggie with me for visits distracted me from the heartache I felt watching our dear Sophia continue to decline.

And three, Sophia's sadness at our departure grew heavier. She began to get teary-eyed when I had to say goodbye. After my last visit, tears flowed heavily from the corners of her eyes, as though she would never see me again. I look back now and realize she knew the end was coming.

Not more than a week after that visit, I came out of the bathroom, all ready for school, to find my aunt sitting across from my mom at our dining room table. My aunt was the school's connection for the Adopt-a-Grandparent program. I knew why she was there, and my heart sank. Mom pushed a chair out from the table, ushering me to sit beside her.

"I'm really sorry to have to share this, Ally, but I got a call this morning. Sophia passed away," my aunt said, her own voice solemn and her eyes tearing up.

Utter devastation. I buried my face in my arms on the table. This was my first experience with death. I hadn't yet lost a relative or a friend. Not even a pet. And while I didn't want Sophia to suffer any longer than she had, I was painfully sad.

"You were so good to her. And I know how much she enjoyed your visits." She looked to my mom from across the table, those few tears falling now slowly down the path along the inside of her nose. My mom placed her hand on my back.

When Sophia's obituary came out a few days later, I barely recognized the woman in the photo. This couldn't possibly be the person I had spent the last two-and-a-half years visiting. The obituary said she was in her mid-50s. The Sophia I had visited looked like she was in her 70s. The obituary talked about all she had accomplished in her life.

The Sophia I had visited couldn't do anything. The obituary listed her family. Never once had I run into them at her residence, or even found evidence of the last time they were there. The one exception in the time I had known her: her son took her out one Saturday afternoon and brought her to see me in *Godspell* (just a handful of months prior to her passing).

I didn't know how to weave it all together. Sophia before her disease and the Sophia after. The here and then not.

What I knew to do was write. I wrote a letter to the editor about the Adopt-a-Grandparent program and why it was important. And I wrote a letter for her family about my relationship with Sophia and what she meant to me. In one part of that letter, I said:

> Sophia was a miracle, an angel sent from God. And my angel has just regained her voice, her spirit, and her life. I will remember and love her forever, and someday our paths will cross again.

But I wish I could get a do-over, because I look back on my relationship with Sophia, and I recognize new lessons I couldn't possibly have understood back then.

Sophia taught me about abled and disabled bodies. About powerlessness and hope. She taught me how to listen, see, and hear others by paying attention, using your other senses, by being present and not turning away. By sitting with someone in their total vulnerability. Sometimes, it doesn't require words. In fact, a lot of the time it doesn't. She taught me about small acts of kindness and small illustrations of love. How you can build trust and intimacy simply by being real and reliable, and by being able to embrace what still *is,* rather than what is no longer.

Through Sophia, I learned about the love inside of friendship, about trust and bonds that are unbreakable. That the right friends, the deepest friends, become family, and those ties can be as strong as (if not stronger than) blood. When Sophia passed, Maggie wrote me this note:

> You will never know how much our friendship means to me. I truly treasure it. The friendship that we share some people spend a lifetime looking for. Sophia was a great woman that, while drawing us closer to her, she brought us closer to each other. I thank God for being able to share the time I would with her, and for the continued time I get to share with you. I love you.

That note stays tucked in my Sophia album, alongside all the pictures I ever sent to Sophia, the letters I wrote her, the cards I sent. There are pictures of me and of Maggie from our semi-formals and proms. Maggie has been my best friend since. I joke and say she's my Wife in Another Life. We know when we are old, widowed by our significant others, we will be on a porch somewhere, rocking together and enjoying the same raucous laughter we always have. We're going on twenty years of friendship, and the depths of it began in Sophia's room, at her side.

Most importantly, Sophia taught me no matter what you can or cannot do, we all matter. I think of Sophia and see resilience and bravery. I see a woman who kept opening her eyes each day, even though the view was bleak. I see a woman who kept going in the face of it all, one breath and one blink at a time. Who still found joy in the smallest of things, while the largest of them lorded over her.

If You ever run into her, tell her I said, "hello, and thank you."

With gratitude for the people in my life, present and past,

A friend of Sophia

QUESTIONS FOR YOUR PATH TO BRAVERY

Who is a person in your life who has taught you powerful lessons?

Actions speak louder than words. What do your own actions say about you? What do the actions of those closest to you say about how they care about you?

Letter 8
CHOOSING WRITING—ACT ONE

Dear Cosmic Conspirator,

If I could summarize adolescence, it was feeling like I was wildly misunderstood. Being in a pressure cooker of activities meant to positively impact the potential for my college acceptance. Dating the wrong guy. And legitimizing my future writing career. I would say three out of the four of these might describe three out of four girls' adolescence. Or at least 3/4th of teenage movies with female protagonists. (Someday I'll expect You to tell me the actual percentage.)

Before college and careers became a consistent topic of conversation, my personal interest and energy in writing projects was of little concern. But once that frequent flyer question *"What are you going to study in college?"* started to circulate, my response—"Writing"— wasn't landing so well.

Writing had been a cute kid's dream when I was eleven and writing really shitty memoirs, but not so cute as a developing teenager who needed to think about her future. (Come to think of it, it may have been how shitty that one memoir was that soured people on the prospect of me leading a writer's life). Being a solid writer would be helpful in college, for things like writing academic papers. Writing was a worthy enough hobby, but it was *not* a career path. Not for me. So said parents, grandparents, adult family friends, and the world-at-large.

You can't make a living from writing.

I suppose it's fair to assume the people who poo-pooed my passion thought about writing in a stereotypical way. The lonely writer, holed up in her house, pounding away at the keyboard until all hours, barely keeping the lights turned on or her belly fed, living in squalor, determined (nay, destined?) to write the next great American novel, which would surely bring her such popularity and fortune as had by Patterson, Grisham, King, or the most renowned (at the time) J.K. Rowling.

They (adults in my life, not famous writers), in their realism, understood these prolific and best-selling authors were in the top 1% of writers, their compatriots a good distance behind them. The other 99% were not making it, or at least not nearly as well.

For me, I didn't see writing as impossible. Perhaps improbable, to reach that level of esteem and recognition, but not so unworthy I would abandon my dreams altogether. As such, I had to fight for it. I had to defend it. And I needed to prove I was good at it. Or excellent, ideally. Because only if I were *excellent* could I make it. That meant I needed others—reputable "others"—to classify my excellence.

My entire childhood, English teachers often told me about writing contests and conferences, knowing my affinity for writing. I took every chance I could to enter. The winter of my sophomore year, a teacher encouraged me to apply for the New England Young Writer's Conference, which took place at Bread Loaf in Middlebury, Vermont, just a couple hours drive from home. But Bread Loaf drew a nationwide applicant pool. Living in Vermont didn't guarantee you a spot. You applied and were judged against all the other high school students from across the U.S. who also wanted to attend. Being invited to the Bread Loaf campus was a VERY. BIG. DEAL.

The Bread Loaf Writers' Conference dates back to 1926. It's the oldest writing conference in America, and still to this day is easily one of the most prestigious of conferences for writers to be admitted to. You make it into Bread Loaf and you're totally legit. (Not to say you're not legit without it; I just mean, *you're recognized*. There's no debating.)

You'll imagine then what a freakin' high it was to receive my acceptance letter early spring. I was officially admitted into an elite group of teenagers, and my talent for writing was confirmed. This meant everything to me. (Thank You by the way. Finally, I felt You were conspiring with me.)

I did have a way with words.

I would grow up to be a writer.

I could make it.

You'll also recall how badly my balloon burst when my dad came into my room to "discuss" the matter of attending Bread Loaf.

There I was, gripping my acceptance letter like the golden ticket into Willy Wonka's Chocolate Factory, sitting on my bedroom floor, reading it over and over again in complete disbelief and exhilaration, and he came in.

"Mom says you got into that young writer's conference thing in Middlebury."

Thing?!

"Bread Loaf," I said with that air of snobbery and disgust that pretty much comes with every line of dialogue ever spoken by a teenage girl to her father.

"It looks like the dates are the same weekend as the prom," he said.

"And?" I asked ripe with attitude. I was fully prepared for the possibility this conversation would nosedive into *you need to be more practical* territory, so I was bracing myself.

"Well wouldn't you like to go?"

"You're assuming I'll be asked. I can't just go as a freshman." He knew this, of course.

"An upper-classmen might ask you. Your sister has been every year because she was asked."

That was true. She *had* been asked to prom every year. She seemed to like going. People seemed to like asking her. I, on the other hand, didn't foresee being asked. I also didn't give a shit.

"I won't be asked by an upper-classmen," I said with an exaggerated eye roll. (You know, 'cause I'm an exaggerator.)

"How do you know that?"

"I'm not friends with any upper-class boys. Nor do I like any of them."

(You'll remember the *wrong guy*—the one who turned out *not* to be 'the one'—didn't enter stage left until later that year. And while we are on *that* topic, let me just be clear: You'll never get a thank you for that guy. I don't care how much I learned, or what I said before about each person coming into our life for a reason.)

"There's still time for that," my dad said. "An upperclassmen could still ask you."

(See, freshmen and sophomores could only go if asked by upperclassmen.)

"Why does prom matter? I can't get anywhere with prom. You spend a bunch of money on a dress you wear once. You dance a bunch like every other school dance. Plus, I've got my junior and senior year to go."

"I don't want you to regret missing out on this, if an invitation arises." (Yes, he put it just like that.)

"Except we don't know an invitation will exist. We *do know* I got into Bread Loaf. And would *rather* go to Bread Loaf. Not prom."

He did that motion with his hands, two palms down toward the ground, pushing the rising air back toward the floor slowly, telling me to *simmer.*

"I'm not trying to upset you or tell you that you can't go. I just want you to think about the pros and cons to each."

What was I not saying? How was I being unclear?

He was my dad, and I just expected him to know what was in my heart. To understand this chance was epic. I wanted him to read my mind and get what was in it.

"Dad. I choose Bread Loaf."

He didn't push after that, and I won.

Ally and Writing—1 point

Parents and Rest of World—0

Except, I felt like shit—at least immediately. The magic of the moment dashed by my dad's inability to 'get it.'

That spring, overlapping prom weekend, I went to Bread Loaf for four wonderful days and slept in a dorm room on a college campus. I spent whole days with other kids whose hearts were filled with stories and poems. Who wanted to change the world with their words. Who were gifted in stringing sentences together. I can still picture our group workshopping our pieces in the grass under an old oak tree. Walking in packs to the main hall, where there were readings every afternoon and evening. Lining up to have books signed by local and national writers who were actualizing the very dreams we all held silently on any normal day. A normal day away from here. At this moment in time, we could wear our W badge boldly and proudly.

I'm still immensely proud of having been selected to attend. To have had that opportunity. To have been recognized in that way. I'm also immensely proud I acted on my dreams, because there came harder times after that when it didn't feel as easy. I didn't feel as bold. Or as brave. I caved a little. Made compromises. Tried to choose win-win solutions that never really worked out. At least not for me. Not in the long run.

I look back now and see how I misplaced my energy on needing proof or permission from others to write, or to excel in writing, or to be recognized as a writer. Everything I needed, I already had inside me. The person whose permission and acceptance I needed was my own.

I look back now, and I see parents and grandparents and adults who didn't want to squash my dreams, but they wanted to prepare me for realities. The reality of student loan debt. Bills. Rents and mortgages. Car payments. Security. Stability. And I wish I hadn't been so snotty. So defensive. But I also wish I could have figured out how to make them see what I felt inside me. What I knew inside me. That way none of us would have doubted. None of us would have been afraid. And we could have communicated a little more clearly what we all wanted for me: happiness (and enough money to eat).

Write on,

The legitimate writer

QUESTiONS FOR YOUR PATH TO BRAVERY

Has there been a time you acted bravely in pursuit of what you really wanted? How did it feel? Would you change how you went about it?

If not, imagine what you would do. What would happen if you went after *that thing* you've been thinking about?

Letter 9
SHE NEEDS TO TALK TO SOMEONE

Dear All Knowing One,

You have always known what I've needed when I needed it the most. I know I haven't always been grateful, especially at the outset, when the hard knocks are happening. I haven't always been able to see You were trying to steer me or offer me something useful. How many times have you heard me say, "Come on?!" or "The Universe can be a real dick sometimes!" (as though You couldn't hear me), when I thought You were throwing more shit my way instead of helping me through it.

I guess it's kind of like that "Footprints in the Sand" poem, where someone is pissed off with Jesus for abandoning them when they needed Him the most, and Jesus is like, "Hey Samantha, I've been here the whole time. See those friggin' footsteps? Those are mine. You've been on my back for miles. Days. Months, even. And you and your burdens are heavy. Did you know that?" Then I imagine the human part of Him mumbles, "So quit your bitching already and throw me a little 'thanks'."

(This is me admitting I've done my fair amount of bitching and not enough 'thanks giving.')

I definitely know I wasn't giving You any credit at sixteen when the pediatrician looked at my mom and said, "She needs to talk to someone." I wasn't about to thank You for calling me crazy and telling me I needed to see "a shrink."

Yet I know it was inevitable. There was no way around it. While I had every intention of figuring out how to stay away from spontaneously combusting after being deemed a Ticking Time Bomb the year before, I had failed to do anything other than internalize *everything.* The expectations of school to get high grades and load my schedule with extracurriculars. The frequent disagreeable conversations about college and what I was going to do with my life. It was like living in a pressure cooker, with my boyfriend and my parents each playing with the dial, trying to get my setting right.

I was in a long-distance relationship with that guy with the less-than-stellar reputation, who was three years older and newly military. My parents had a strong distaste for him that was evident, even if they never said "We hate him" out loud.

He felt the same way about them.

They were each convinced the other was wrong for me. Either he didn't get me, or they didn't. While there may have been ample evidence on either side, as soon as one insulted the other, my defenses flew up. They were my parents. How dare he insult them. He was my boyfriend—the love of my life, at the time (the guy I thought I'd be with forever—You know the unfortunate way teenagers think about their first loves). How come they couldn't just be supportive? He wasn't *that bad,* was he, from thousands of miles away? (That's a hypothetical question. Don't answer that.) I felt loyalty to both sides. I couldn't choose.

Deepening the chasm between love and family was the chasm between love and church, caused by my heat-of-the-moment decision to lose my virginity. I certainly wasn't the only teenager *doing it,* but my parents didn't know—or at least I hadn't told them. What about my Catholic upbringing? Was I now destined for hell? What kept me from losing it (my mind, not my virginity, obviously) was believing he was "the one". We would marry. So, save *it* for later or don't. What was the difference? (This was my brain 'on adolescence'.)

The perspective worked…until it didn't.

There did come a day of reckoning when I looked at myself in the mirror and thought, "Oh, God, what have I done?" A time when I came to realize he was not Mr. Forever, and I wanted to take my "eggs and basket" back, finally understanding my mother's sage advice on love. I entered a deep internal place of regret, shame, and self-loathing that I didn't dare speak out loud. (Do You give every adolescent girl this virginity turmoil? Because it blows.) But that day of reckoning and recognition of regret came later—*after* working with a therapist.

The lies, secrecy about my "choices," the void between him and my parents, schoolwork and my extracurricular load, all were weighing me down. Add to all of this the pressure I felt to live up to a public perception of my last name, living in a small town where everyone knew us because of my dad's profession—in the dairy industry (a very big deal in rural VT)—and both my parents' high-profile involvement in our community. (I know. Apple, meet Tree.) It was all TOO much, and it came barreling down on me even while I struggled to clearly identify any one of these as the source to my stress.

What I did know was I got eight or more hours of sleep at night, but still felt exhausted. I woke up mornings with such apathy for school. I had persistent headaches. Was crying in the shower for reasons I couldn't articulate.

Education and life have since taught me I was dealing with depression and anxiety, but I didn't know it then. My parents worried that something was terribly wrong (physically). After eliminating the eye problems—the presumption that my headaches were caused by a sight problem, a fair enough conclusion since both my parents wear glasses—the next stop was our pediatrician.

I felt far too old to be walking into his office.

Even worse, circus images bordered every wall in the examining room, and bright lollipops and Looney Tune stickers were readily available on the countertops for young patients who followed the doctor's instructions or were brave when getting their flu shot.

The sound of white exam-table paper crunched under my weight as I followed instructions and hoisted myself onto the table. The normal checks—throat, eyes, heart, lungs, blood pressure. All normal. Then he leaned back against the cabinets. He crossed one brown-tweed leg over the other, revealing high, brown socks. He crossed one arm across his chest, hiding portions of his red striped suspenders. The other arm angled up toward his chin, his fingers combing through his beard.

He scanned my face for just a moment. That one look. He knew what I didn't.

"How's school?" he asked.

"Fine," I shrugged, but I could already feel that swell in my throat inflating, like the air that comes into a frog's neck right before it bellows. That swell was either going to burst forward into ugly sobs or turn into a giant cotton ball and choke out the sound of my voice altogether.

"What about home, or your relationships?"

If sobs were substance instead of sound, I would have doused him so heavily his tweed slacks would have sagged off his suspenders, and his shoes would have sloshed with every step.

Had I not been crying so violently, I would have felt shame, because even then, I knew I didn't have it *that bad*. I knew others elsewhere were truly suffering. Without homes or food. Without family or love. Diagnosed with terrible diseases. Bullied for being different. Discriminated against for the color of their skin or their sexual orientation.

So much pain in the world. What could I possibly be this upset about?

Yet, there I was. I couldn't deny my exhaustion, or my headaches. Or the fact something very serious was the matter, even if I couldn't find the words.

I can't recall what he asked next. I just remember my mother being brought in while I was still sniveling on the exam table, her figure blurry through my tears.

"Physically, everything checks out fine," the doctor said. "But she needs to talk to someone."

My mother looked at him as though she didn't understand.

"I have a therapist that works from this office a couple days a week. She's great with adolescents. The receptionist can give you her information at the front, as you check out. I would start there and see if her physical symptoms improve."

And that is truly when the shame sank in.

Not only was I upset about elements of my life I couldn't even name nor justify, but I had to see a shrink. Which meant I was crazy, because with little actual knowledge of the world, I knew therapists were only for crazy people. I didn't know the term *mentally ill,* yet. Nor did I have any true understanding or compassion for those who suffered from mental illness—I had never met anyone with a diagnosis or disorder. At least not yet, not to my knowledge.

Topping it off, the doctor's prescription to talk to a therapist seemed to land on my mother's ears as though she had failed me. Which eventually transferred to my father, when he was told "the prescription." What other explanation could there be for their child's need to talk to someone who wasn't them?

This was the assumption I made. The look on my mother's face while the doctor told her. The way she tried to pry out of me what was bothering me on the car ride home—a question I couldn't even begin to answer. The way my father did the same. Both desperate to get me to speak. To share. To divulge.

"What aren't you telling us? What are you hiding? What is bothering you so deeply?"

As a parent now, I totally get what rose in their chests was panic. Fear. Overwhelm. Had there been a physical diagnosis, we all could treat it with some medication, or physical therapy, or exercise. We'd be on a concrete road to recovery.

But feelings and thoughts, ones I couldn't yet articulate, were ambiguous. Unclear. No one knew what was happening, whose fault it was, how it could be resolved. Whatever *it* was. I'm sure they were thinking, "We've done the best we could. We've tried to give her everything. What is going on?" (Also, I'm sure they were thinking, "It's *that boy.*" I mean, what parent wouldn't?)

With my own son, I worry about whether there will be a time when he doesn't feel he can come to me to speak about what bears down on him. When he doesn't feel he can sit and try to express some thought or emotion he's grappling with. While I know I'll be able to suggest he talk to a therapist, because of my own experience, I also know I'll wonder what I failed to do to ensure he felt he could talk to me. Because I, too, am doing the best I can to give him all he needs. I, too, would be wondering and worrying, "What is happening?"

But I couldn't find the words they wanted to hear at that time. I truly didn't know what was causing me such melancholy, such overwhelm. I hadn't asked to feel exhausted. I hadn't asked for the headaches. I hadn't wanted to feel weepy. I certainly didn't want to feel ungrateful. Or make them feel like failures. It was just there—this family of white elephants, one on each of our chests, and others sitting on the couch in every room.

Now I see it was years coming on. Starting back at age ten, when my teacher remarked I took on too much. A slow, subtle boil.

But thank you, Universe. You got me where I needed to be. Inside that pediatrician's office.

That five-word sentence, "She needs to talk to someone," very well may have saved my life. Not because I was suicidal, but because I could have very well continued in the way I had been. Which undeniably would have ended in a nervous breakdown.

"She needs to talk to someone" became one of the most critical moments of my life.

I met Celia. My therapist. The person even now, in my thirties, I seek out for emotional excavating and repair. And Celia introduced me to talk therapy, EMDR (eye movement desensitization and reprocessing), visualization, and self-care. She encouraged my journaling. She encouraged my self-advocacy.

Through Celia, I learned about psychology and mental health, two areas that became academic and professional pursuits, when I finally caved and agreed to study something other than writing. They were fascinating subjects that provided wonderful shading and layering and perspectives about the world and people. Most importantly, in working with Celia, I was invited to speak my truth in a safe space and be heard. To be seen. Separate from my family, my relationship, my community. Just me. As I was.

What liberation.

Beyond my own personal development, "She needs to talk to someone" had a powerful ripple effect. In releasing my inner turmoil in a safe space, I had more room to breathe and strengthen my better qualities. This meant I showed up differently at school and at home. In showing up differently in these places, others showed up differently for me. Celia had told me, in systems theory, the idea is, when one of us changes, it impacts the rest. Our action or response influences the action or response of people around us. It's this beautiful dance, the intricate inner workings of a finely tuned clock.

"She needs to talk to someone" became my entry point to self-care, self-awareness, and self-love, which I've discovered (repeatedly because, as You and I both know, I don't always learn what I need to the first time) is the foundation for any success. You must take care of yourself first. You must release and express rather than hold it inside where it festers and spoils you from the inside out. We all need to speak. We all need to be heard. We all need to shed the extra weight that drags us down. With that comes clarity, perspective, and, even, freedom.

With deepest thanks for giving me the platform for speaking honestly and openly (even though I was really whiny about it initially),

Your continually-evolving-but-pretty-well-adjusted -as-an-adult Ally

QUESTIONS FOR YOUR PATH TO BRAVERY

What do you need to say, or what do you need to shed, that you've
been holding on to for too long?

Identify a time you chose to respond differently and how it
impacted the greater system around you?

Letter 10
THESE ARE *NOT* MY PEOPLE

Dear Perfect Celestial Being,

You must recognize how flawed people are. How could you not? Does it ever get to be just too much? Do You chat with God about how messed up we all are? There are so many times I wonder how can *me* and *that guy over there* both be considered a part of the same race, when we couldn't be further apart.

The first time I remember feeling devastatingly like *these are not my people* was when "Take Back Vermont" signs took over my hometown. They seemed to crop up overnight.

One morning we were driving down the same street we always drove on to go to school, but these yard signs were everywhere. They were nonsensical to me. *Where had Vermont gone? Who had taken it?*

"What's with the signs?" I asked. "What do they mean?"

My dad explained in the most politically correct way possible. "Those folks who oppose gay marriage believe Vermont is heading in the wrong direction, if we allow people of the same sex to join in Civil Unions that grant them the same rights as married couples."

Translation: anti-gay people had placed picket signs on their lawns to loudly and proudly claim their straight way was the only way.

When we turned off the first street and onto the next, it was clear this intolerance had taken over the town—a majority of the lawns bore signage.

"But why do people care if a man marries a man?"

"Some people feel that marriage is a sacred bond between man and woman," Dad said, and we both glanced out the window at the Catholic church as we drove by.

Aren't there worse things people can do than love each other? I wondered.

"But isn't Jesus all about love? Who cares with who? There are worse things," I responded.

My dad remained silent.

And isn't there supposed to be a separation of Church and State? But I didn't ask that out loud.

Clearly, I was missing something that would make this make sense. There must have been more, for this many people in town to all be on the same side.

But there wasn't. While I already had gripes with small town culture—gossip wheels and everyone knowing everything (or thinking they knew everything) about everyone else, and our family getting hate mail anytime one of us was mentioned in the paper for doing something "newsworthy"—this took my derision to a whole new level. Asking myself *"What was wrong with people?"* turned into, *"These are not my people."* I wanted to disown the town altogether. My first act toward doing so would be to get out as soon as I could.

Shortly after the pickets took over the towns, the Allied Spaces signs went up in the school outside the guidance counselor's doors, and in some of the teachers' classrooms. Quickly, I learned these signs signified welcoming places for gay students. The acronym LGBTQ, or its individual terms, were still foreign to me. What I knew, or what my community wanted me to believe, was: there was gay, and there was straight, and only one was right.

I had seen this play out at school, a subset of the greater community as a whole.

In high school, if you weren't overtly and stereotypically straight, then you *must* be gay. It was that straightforward (no pun intended). It was that narrow minded. That stupid. But also, that ruthless.

If you were too artistic...

Wore too much black...

Were too 'flamboyant'...

Too single...

Had too many 'girlfriends'...

You were Gay.

Such was the reality for Grant, my classmate, who became one of my best friends. While my adolescence may have been one of feeling misunderstood and out of place, and fighting for my dreams to write, his was being bullied and fighting to defend himself against our peers' *perceptions* (and disdain) that he was 'gay,' because he didn't contort himself to the confines of masculine gender norms. He didn't play a lot of sports, hang out with a lot of dudes, or physically objectify a bunch of girls.

His teen years could be summed up as constantly reporting harassment to the administration, and getting ineffective or no response. Despite his mother advocating for him, despite her working for the school, no one helped him. In fact, a principal said to him,

"Stop asking for it."

These were not my people.

The harassment went beyond the school hallways or grounds. One afternoon after school, Grant was beaten up in an old marble mill tucked into a corner of town. After being chased home, there was no denying what had happened. His mother took him and his freshly purpled eye to the local police station. Grant told the police who had attacked him.

"Yeah. That kid is bad news. We're looking into him for other things." That was it. That was supposed to bring the feeling of safety or justice to my friend.

These were not my people.

Grant wasn't the only classmate suffering at the hands of our peers. There were at least two other students who easily stood out as targets because of their mannerisms, or because of the alternative ways they dressed or did their hair. I imagine they, too, had been told, "Stop asking for it."

Simultaneously, Reid, a dark-skinned senior who had been adopted from India in his youth, and who hadn't lost all of his native accent, was also being harassed. For him, it wasn't the word 'gay,' but the 'n' word.

Reid was being called the 'n' word at any available opportunity by a kid, Chase, known for being a brute and a bully. Chase's hatred was relentless. Reid repeatedly reported the harassment, and also went without effective response. I watched him in the halls, time and again, walking away from the word you could see slashing through him at each jab. I watched as his friends surrounded him, encouraging him not to throw punches (likely knowing Chase would do serious damage, as Reid was no match in height or weight.)

Then one day, normal cafeteria chatter and laughter and the sound of chip bags being opened, dishes clattering in the kitchen, all was disrupted by screams, fast movements, and blood across the floor.

Reid had heard the 'n' word for the very last time. He'd grabbed the crutch from underneath Chase's arm (acquired from a recent four-wheeling escapade gone wrong) and bashed him over the head until he drew blood.

Teachers swarmed in. Students scattered. Palms covered mouths. Wide eyes stared at every turn.

While the fact that blood had been drawn probably should have given me even the slightest concern for Chase, all I felt was he had gotten what he deserved. I still don't know if that makes me a bad person—to have had such little care it was Chase's blood on the floor. I know I would have felt differently if Reid had been the one injured.

At that moment, I looked at Reid and saw an iteration of a ticking time bomb, except it was one that had attempted to disarm itself with reporting and seeking support, but to no avail. Who could Reid speak to, if no one here listened? What else was he supposed to do, when he was already saying all he needed to say, but no one heard him? He was screaming into a crowded room as though he were entirely mute. The answer for him: take care of it himself.

While Reid applied his own justice, the school applied an immediate suspension with the threat of expulsion. The threat of not being allowed to attend his Senior prom. The threat of not graduating. The threat of assault charges. All of those were a threat to his eligibility to enlist in the military—the one opportunity he was counting on as his ticket out of here after graduation.

Just like Take Back Vermont had divided our community, so did this singular event.

You either stood with Reid, or you stood with Chase.

I chose my side swiftly, having learned on the playground all those years ago that sometimes there is no place for neutral. You choose. You pick a side. (See, I do learn from my experiences. Thank You very much.)

When an afterschool protest of students gathered in Reid's favor, to support allowing him to attend prom and graduation, I walked in the circle the silent students made in the middle of the cafeteria, where blood had so recently sprinkled the white-and-blue checkered linoleum. It was my first deliberate act of advocacy. Of justice. Of being a representative for someone else who had been ignored. To make a point for someone else whose voice apparently didn't matter. While our protest was silent, it was powerful. It was seen. It was heard. Unlike Reid had been.

Reid was allowed to attend prom. He was allowed to graduate. The wild and raucous applause that resulted as he stepped onto stage to get his diploma was incredible. A victory. I still get goosebumps when I think about him, up there in his royal blue robe and cap, his wide, ear-to-ear smile.

While Reid got to graduate, Grant, my 'gay' friend, still had another year to endure. I'd like to say the harassment waned for him, but it simply morphed. From overt verbal attacks to gossip and whispers that were still heard and very much felt. He was encouraged by a guidance counselor to join the Gay Straight Alliance, as though by becoming an ally, would somehow curb the perception (and the bullying) about his sexual orientation. What really seemed to happen was, the more he involved himself in extracurriculars, the more he could be surrounded by people who really knew him, and the voices of friends drowned out the others.

He survived. We graduated. And we both chose colleges outside of Vermont. We both were desperate to experience other places. Thinking, in going somewhere else, our troubles would somehow be gone.

I refused to apply to in-state schools. I had to get away from this place full of people who I could not claim as my own. This small mindedness. I had assumed the entire state resembled the microcosm I grew up in. I had this unrealistic and naïve belief that *anywhere else* must be better, more progressive. A sheltered viewpoint, of course. I saw the community like the townspeople with pitchforks in *Beauty and the Beast*, ready to storm the castle. These were not my people, and so I had no choice but to leave. It felt like you either joined them or weren't one of them. A binary situation. Neither suited me. So, I would go out of state for college and leave it all behind.

I headed to liberal arts college in the Midwest, and Grant took off for a liberal arts college in Massachusetts. We were both determined to start over. Find new people—*our people*—and find ourselves.

Just before Thanksgiving break, Grant called me from his bathroom floor. I hadn't talked to him in months.

"Hey, friend! How are you?" I picked up, excited to hear his voice and catch up.

"I have to tell you something." His voice shook.

"Okay."

"But I'm worried how you'll take it."

I couldn't imagine what he was about to reveal, but I could hear the fear in his voice.

"Well, tell me, and then we'll talk through it."

He paused. Then sniffled.

I waited.

"I'm gay."

I was in disbelief. Had we not just spent all of high school defending his heterosexuality? I knew so little about repression, or coming out, or being gay. And how was it all those terrible people had perceived something he himself deeply denied, and I, as one of his best friends, never saw or thought?

"Ally?"

I hadn't realized I had stopped talking.

"Sorry…I'm here."

"Are you upset?"

"Of course not." To that I could reply quickly, honestly, but then I took another pause, trying to determine what to say to him.

"I'm worried for you, though."

This time he was silent.

"I don't feel like it's going to be easy for you," I finished my thought.

I couldn't offer anything else. I wanted to be comforting. Reassuring. But high school wasn't that far removed. The bullying wasn't that far removed. Take Back Vermont wasn't that far removed. The world was still so cruel, so judgmental, so intolerant. While I wanted my friend to be every ounce of himself, I was also terrified.

"Thank you," he said and his voice relaxed. He shifted into relief.

"For what?"

"For being honest. That's the first *real* response I've gotten. Everyone else has been all, like, 'I knew it.' Or, 'Duh.' And then, like,

'So what else is new?' Or, 'Is that it?' Like, why am I even calling them."

People can kind of suck sometimes. See. We've come full circle.

"That sucks…if it makes you feel any better, I had no idea this is what you were going to say?" I laughed.

"Really?"

"Really. Maybe I just never cared about that. Whether you like men or women. Who gives a shit? You're still you."

We caught up as usual. We hung up. And then as I feared, the next however many years were incredibly hard. For both of us, actually, except I had only predicted them for him, because he was gay and I had already seen how people treated him when it was only their perception. I often wondered, in those first few years after he came out, whether he remained closeted in high school because he was already being treated so badly. What more might have happened, if he had come out then and waved his pride flag?

Now, we're mid-thirties, and we still think of each other as best friends. We don't talk every day. We don't see each other that often. But we have always been there through the worst of the worst. We've talked in the middle of the night when one of us needs the other desperately. We've cried together. We've shared dark humor to get us through dark patches. We've had each other's backs. And we've also celebrated each other's journeys, because it hasn't always been so depressing; we've both come out on the other side.

I've seen him, always. In all his awesomeness, and in all his struggle. He's seen me in mine. It hasn't mattered where I've gone, or where he was. He has remained *my people* for bearing witness to all parts of me and accepting and loving me anyway, and I've remained his for all the same.

It's not geography. It's not small town versus big city. It's shared beliefs, ideas, and values that bind you to the people who matter to you most. It's mutual love and respect. When you come to find those you align with the most, it makes choosing a stance and picking a side feel easy and feel right. When you've found *your people,* that can transcend state borders or town lines, and there's a little more hope for humanity and a little more pride toward your place within it.

Thanks for the awesome people on the planet I can claim as mine,

One of the awesome ones

QUESTIONS FOR YOUR PATH TO BRAVERY

What are the qualities of *your* people?

With whom or where do you feel you most belong?

Letter 11
ON LIVING AND DYING

Dear Un-Understandable Universe,

This I won't ever 'get': why my college roommate died. Will You ever explain *that* to me? Will it ever make sense?

I mean, I feared death even before that happened. Maybe we all do as humans. Fear our own mortality. Some might say, in that fear is the will to live. To make the most out of life.

Perhaps I always feared it, but I don't recall ever talking about it. Not outside of the understanding that, when you die, you go to heaven. (Or so you hope.) Perhaps because I was fortunate to go through most of my youth without knowing anyone close to me who *did* die. Sophia was the one exception, but she was ill, and her death, when it came, seemed like mercy.

But, Kaitlyn?

To this day, I can't wrap my head around it. I know she's not the only nineteen-year-old to leave the world unexpectedly and unfairly. Shortly after she passed, a high school classmate was defeated by leukemia. Not long after her, one of my brother's classmates died in a tragic car accident. None of these made sense. They were all too much to bear.

I know life isn't fair, but that's not a good enough answer. And if that *is* the answer, You really are an asshole sometimes.

A letter from a family friend, who wrote to me at the time Kaitlyn passed, says, "There are the questions. Why? Why her? Why not someone else? Questions for which there are no answers. Except to say, it was her time, even though she was too young."

I'll get behind "it was her time," but I still wanna know why. Why was it her time?

I look back on my relentless pursuit to attend that liberal arts school in Ohio, feeling so deeply it was the place I was meant to be, and I wonder...

As soon as I received the first marketing brochure with its motto "Accent on the Individual," I knew I wanted to go there. Felt called to be there. I thought it was because I could study both psychology and creative writing, and because, with its focus on individuality, I could reinvent myself. A place where no one knew me as a ticking time bomb, or by my last name, or as the girl who dated that boy with the bad reputation.

When my mom took me on a college tour and we visited the campus, I felt that pull again to be there. One meeting with a creative writing professor solidified my desires to attend and to write under his tutelage. I loved walking across the quad. I loved the gigantic courtyard clocks that were perfectly placed. The tacky purple-and-gold eagle statues outside of every building, each with its own name, if you looked hard enough to find them.

Deep inside, I had the feeling I was supposed to be there. You gave me that distinctive knowing, like the knowing I had about writing.

Was it because I was meant to witness this event?

My first undergraduate year, You introduced me to a bright-eyed, altruistic, idealistic, authentic, down-to-earth young woman I couldn't wait to make my bosom friend. I thought for sure she would be the Diana Barry to my Anne Shirley. You gave us the opportunity to scheme over the next summer and swap our roommates so we could room together for our sophomore year instead.

I was over the moon with excitement that Kaitlyn and I would spend our evenings staying up late, talking and laughing. Getting involved in the same activities. Introducing each other to our parents on family weekend. I relished the idea our bond would grow so tightly that, eventually, we would be bridesmaids in each other's wedding. Present at each other's baby showers. Calling each other when we faced mom-life and were totally unsure of ourselves. And escaping it all by meeting up every year for a girl's weekend.

Finally, Sophomore year began. We didn't see each other as much as I'd envisioned, since we were both overly involved on campus and carried full course loads, but I loved the passing catchups, as one of us came and the other went. The intermittent chatter during the rare occasions we both were in our room doing schoolwork. I hold on to the memory of the floor activity, hosted by our resident assistant, when we got to make signs for our doors (Kaitlyn created a golf-themed sign for her high-school-turned-college sweetheart.) Or the time she, I, and a few other girls on our floor sang at the top of our lungs to the "Moulin Rouge" soundtrack before piling onto a lower bunk to take photos together.

It all started off so sweetly.

Then, not even a full month into the semester, I was in my boyfriend's dorm room, waking up to the sound of sirens. Ambulance.

It was early on a Tuesday morning. I felt a jarring ping of knowing.

Panic crept into my chest and my throat went dry. Those sirens were too close. They were *on campus*. I resisted the urge to run, even though it was strong, because we still had an hour or two remaining before co-ed visitation hours were open and I could be seen in an all-boys dorm. That time lying awake, staring at the ceiling, wondering what was happening, felt so long. When the clock finally struck eight, I rushed out of his room, unable to explain the feeling in my gut.

When I reached my room, cards and signs were already piling up outside. They were taped to the walls. They were hung with magnets beneath the peep hole on the door. They were propped against wall and door, and some partially slid underneath.

I stared, unable to move.

Kaitlyn.

Our frantic and bewildered resident assistant, mascara tracing paths down her cheeks, tripped over a chair as she made her way toward me. Her trembling lips attempted to shape the words, to recount the morning's event.

An accident. Too much a freak accident. I stared at her, listening, but not sure this could be real.

She told me Kaitlyn fell in the shower and cracked her head open. The girls showering next to her tried to help, but there was so much blood pooling into the drain, and Kaitlyn was unconscious.

The sirens.

For that first day, our floor mates, her boyfriend, and the entirety of campus held on to hope. And there was some. Kaitlyn had stitches, and at some point after arriving at the hospital, she regained consciousness. She even joked with her parents about what a klutz she was. Through the grapevine, we heard she had stubbed her foot on our dorm room door, and in the bathroom, she noticed it was bleeding. The site of the blood made her woozy, and she passed out. We had no reason to believe that wasn't true, or that she wouldn't come back.

But the next morning (Wednesday), there was a totally different reality. Kaitlyn was flown to a Cleveland hospital by helicopter after a blood clot was discovered at the base of her brain. She underwent an extremely high-risk procedure to dissolve the clot—the only possible chance she had. Wednesday evening, the chair of the neurosurgery department informed the family the procedure was ineffective. She had suffered a massive stroke and would never wake up.

Back on campus, we all waited—hours and hours—to hear the news, still hanging on to hope. I went to my normal Wednesday evening meeting for a campus activities group I belonged to, thinking I might have a moment's distraction. Before the meeting ended, the Residence Life coordinator stepped in and asked me to come with her. She brought me to the Vice President for Student Affairs's office, where several other adults stood around the perimeter of the room. Some faces I knew; others, I didn't. A scan of the room, though, and I knew the news was bleak.

Every person's eyes teared. Every person's breath seemed suspended, as though in holding their breath, they would be invisible to me. One single, deep-seated leather chair sat empty in the middle of the semi-circle across from the Vice President's desk.

"Please sit," the Vice President said softly, and she pushed a box of tissues in my direction.

Adults began to dab their eyes and grab each other's hands. My body went cold as I found my way onto the leather cushion.

"We've already notified your parents…"

Notified my parents?

Her voice trailed off into a smattering of words …*"surgery … blood clot … all around the world … unsuccessful … stroke … brain dead … never wake up."*

After that, all I could hear were bellowing sobs that echoed into the high ceilings and reverberated off the tall bookcases and windows. Those sounds were coming from me. Sounds I had never heard before. Every one of my muscles tightened, and yet I shook so badly, it took two adults to hold me steady while her words, this reality, took over my entire body.

It took two more adults to help me walk back to my dorm building, where the same team of people delivered the news to the girls on our floor. I remained around the corner from our hall until the message was given, and then went and sat against the wall near my room, dropping to the carpet as friends flocked to my side and threw their heads in my lap, or grabbed my hands and arms with theirs. A dog pile of wailing young women.

I found myself no longer crying as they wept into my jeans, but whispering the "Our Father" over and over and over again, until my friends could calm their breathing enough to join me.

That night, we all slept together on the floor outside my room. I slept across my door's threshold. My feet inside the room that used to be hers and mine. My head outside in the common area. They slept on blankets on top of the hard floor, their pillows forming a half moon just beyond my door. We slept with our hands stretched into the middle of the circle, folded over each other, in some kind of silent pact. A safe circle, but invincible no more.

The following day brought no miracle. Instead, sometime that afternoon, Kaitlyn's parents made the decision to take her off life support. Shortly after, so we were told, she was gone.

A new theory circulated days after her death. Kaitlyn may have had an aneurism that led to the fall which led to what cascaded after. It was never clear. There was no autopsy, so far as I ever knew. Even if we had been able to pinpoint what caused her fall or her death, it still wouldn't make any sense to me why some of our lives end so early, while others get to live long.

Nothing in this world could have prepared me for this event, and nothing has entirely healed my heart. Sixteen years later, and I am still overwhelmed remembering that week. I still weep when I hear "On Eagle's Wings," or any song from *Moulin Rouge*. I still see September come around and receive the flashes of memory that come with it. I still post R.I.P. messages on the anniversary of her death, and if I have the time, I watch *Peter Pan* in her honor—her favorite Disney movie.

We were nineteen. You aren't supposed to die at nineteen.

We had the world in front of us. We had huge dreams.

I don't understand how You decide. Why was she taken, but I was left behind? Or any of the rest of us?

Why her? Why then? What did it mean?

Tell me. Please.

Am I meant for something bigger here? Or was she meant for something greater There?

Kaitlyn's was the first wake I ever attended. While I wanted to skip going up to the casket to pay my last respects, my father urged me to go. To have one final look at her, and make peace. To honor her life and our friendship. And to place within the casket the photos I had brought of her with me and our friends—pictures we had taken the night of the *Moulin Rouge* sing-along. Five girls, all wearing our Alma Mater hoodies, had leaned into each other on a lower bunk in the dorm so we could squeeze all of us into the photo, while the soundtrack had swirled around us at obnoxious volume.

While I remember her smile from the one picture I kept and framed, my last memory of her is how she looked lying there in a casket, her skin stretched, shiny and waxed, cheeks rouged, blond hair perfectly straight to her shoulders and tucked behind her ears.

It was as though she were a life-size doll.

It was Kaitlyn, and yet it was not. For quick seconds, I thought I could still see her chest rise and fall with breath. I wanted to reach in, grab her by the shoulders, and shake her awake. Instead, I reached for her hand. I placed mine over hers and felt as though my heart fell to my feet and then burst under my weight.

I left the photos and mumbled a few words. Just as the last sounds left my lips, my final goodbye spoken, some other foreign sound rose into my throat, just audible enough for my dad to hear. My body began to drop. My father's arms went up under mine and around my chest. He half carried me, half dragged me away from the casket and into an adjoining room before my ratcheting breath could draw the eyes of everyone in line.

He sat me in a chair, got on his knees, and drew my face into his shoulder, whispering in my ear:

"Breathe."

While I had attended Sophia's funeral, it was as though it had never happened. The unexpectedness of Kaitlyn's death was like a sinkhole, swallowing all who showed up that day, filling the entirety of the church. I couldn't make a guess how many were in attendance. Rows and rows of black-clad bodies. Sniffles and sobs climbing higher and higher into the air. I held tightly to my father's arm, as though I were five-years-old again and terrified of the boogeyman. I was terrified, all right, but it was Death that snatched at the ankles of children.

Kaitlyn's was the first eulogy I ever wrote. The details around how I was asked are fuzzy, but the request was one I couldn't refuse. It was the most tragic of honors. What I do remember is trying to collect thoughts from my friends and dorm mates. All of us unable to come up with any words or thoughts that seemed to do her justice.

I remember my temper flaring and snapping at my father when he attempted to provide ideas or directions, while I sat staring blankly at the computer. Angry tears ran down my face, and I pounded my fist into my dorm-room desk, wondering how on earth I could ever capture her perfectly.

Dad left me to go back to his hotel, recognizing there was nothing he could do to help me write this. He kissed me gingerly on the head. "I know that whatever you end up writing will come straight from the heart, and that is what matters the most."

And then he shut the door quietly, leaving me with her empty chair pushed in under her desk. Her phone buzzed to life with a new message. The sound of the vibration of her phone on the desktop set my teeth on edge. I began to weep quietly.

It was the first time I had ever read or spoken in church, outside of a youth mass. The first time I'd ever stared into a crowd, prepared to speak for some reason that wasn't an artistic or educational endeavor. It was the first time I'd written parting words that weren't for the privacy of the family, as I had when Sophia passed.

"Take your time. Stop and breathe when you need to," Dad whispered one last time, when my name was called to come to the altar. My knees nearly buckled as I passed my dear friend in the closed casket.

How can she actually be in there?

At the podium, I stared into row after row of grief. I stared into faces completely overwhelmed with life's hardest reality: death does not discriminate based on age.

Kaitlyn's parents, her sister, her boyfriend sat in the front pew, red eyed, fallen but not falling apart. And if they weren't falling apart, I couldn't. They looked at me. They waited.

Everyone looked at me. Everyone waited.

I could feel my heart pounding inside my tightened chest. My palms, my armpits, the inside of my thighs, all sweat even though it was cold inside the church and damp outside. I licked my lips, desperate to recover any moisture that might help me speak.

I looked at my dad. He rocked subtly, heel to toe, hands in his pockets, as he always did when standing in Church. Then I looked down at the paper, the words all blurry, until the first few teardrops fell and cleared my vision.

Please, God, let this be good enough for everyone. Especially her.

"'Most people walk in and out of your life. Only friends leave footprints on your heart,'" I began. "Looking out and seeing how many people are here is evidence of how amazing Kaitlyn was and how many people will miss her presence. How someone only 19 could have touched this many lives is unbelievable. But she has."

Somehow, I managed all the way through it. I didn't wail. I didn't pass out. It was slow, labored. My voice was pinched and shook, but I got through. A week later, I was asked to read it again at a memorial service on campus for all those students who were unable to attend the funeral.

Again, I found myself begging for it to be good enough. To have what I said matter somehow. A few weeks later a card arrived from

Kaitlyn's family with this note:

> We know how hard it had to be for you to speak at her funeral
> and service at school. You really brought out her personality
> and you can never know how important that was for us to hear.
> Her sister was afraid no one would talk about her who really
> knew her, and you did that to perfection. We will treasure the
> way you honored her.

I'd like to say that at the time, this brought solace. Comfort. Relief.
But the only thing it did was make me feel like I at least didn't screw
up that part. I regretted not being there the morning she fell. I regretted
by the time I got to the hospital later that day, she had fallen back
asleep. That I missed the last time I would ever have to speak to her. I
realize now how important it was to her family, the way I spoke of her.
But then, those words were not enough to ease an ounce of my grief,
and I didn't trust my words really did that for them, either.

Nothing would ever again be the same.

Not my sense of life and death. Of longevity. Or security.

I was not invincible.

I was not guaranteed a long life.

I was not guaranteed the people I held closest to me would be
around for as long as I wanted them to be.

There was no such thing as control.

I suppose, however, out of that life-death experience also came
gratitude and being present. As a result of her passing, of bearing
witness to her grieving family, I assessed my own relationships to
my parents and siblings. I needed to hold them tighter and closer. We
didn't know when our time would be up. That year at Christmas, I
wrote them each a letter. They *had to know* I loved them.

So, too, were the lessons of strength and resiliency, though it was less obvious at the time. The grief and trauma were too thick. But certainly, to write and deliver my friend's eulogy took strength. To continue to show up in the world, to class, among my peers, even while knowing campus observed me as the "girl whose roommate died," took resilience. To continue to live even while knowing I could die tomorrow, took guts. To truly accept that time was the only ease on grief, took patience. But even with all these lessons learned, I still can't understand *why*.

That picture of Kaitlyn and me on the bottom bunk is framed and sitting on a shelf in my living room. A reminder to myself to see each day as a gift. A reminder to tell the people closest to me, I love them. A reminder even on the worst of days, I still have breath in my lungs.

This past year on the sixteenth anniversary of her death, it just so happened Kay saw that picture for the first time. He recognized me immediately, but not her.

"Who's that?" he asked and pointed at Kaitlyn's smiling face. A smile one teacher was quoted saying, *"Not just a polite smile, but an isn't-life-fabulous smile."*

"That was mommy's friend. She's now in heaven."

"She's my friend, too, then…right?" He looks at me for assurance.

"That's right," I say and force a smile of my own, even though part of my heart tears at that poorly patched seam.

I do hope she's up There with You, looking out for me. Looking out for Kay. I hope she sees I'm trying to honor the gifts I received from her passing. That I'm trying to do right by the life I have been granted. The years I've been allowed to live. The opportunities I've been allowed to experience. I know I have lost my way at times. But I hope from wherever she is, she sees I've done all I can to be the best I can be, so when my time is up, I have no regrets. So when my time is up, people will speak of me the way we all did of her.

With a heavy heart,

The roommate who lived

QUESTIONS FOR YOUR PATH TO BRAVERY

What do you want people to say about how you lived your life?
Are you leading that life now?

At what moment(s) have you showed up braver and more resilient
than you believed yourself to be?

Letter 12
IN THE FACE OF DARKNESS

Hey You,

You have this brilliant poeticism where you bring themes full circle. In looking back on this winding road, I see so many little loops that closed themselves. I'm sure that was by Your design. Like the summer of 2005, I was back home, and I had three internships.

You'll recall I was determined to get into a Ph.D. program for psychology, and I wanted my graduate school application to be rich with so many other accomplishments (yes, AI rearing its ugly head) that no low GRE scores could even make a dent in my chances. As such, I had spent my spring break interviewing at three local placements suggested by my dad, so I would be all set for the summer. Finally, I recognized the power of "it's all about who you know." How many times had I heard him talk about how important your connections could be? Now I was bearing the fruit of his labor.

One of those places was the geriatric facility where Sophia had lived. I hadn't been back there since, and just the thought of it made my "heart sad" (as Kay now says), but the advantage of it was it was familiar. The other was the community mental health agency. Right next door to the offices where I first began seeing Celia and first started to understand mental health. Except I had never noticed it was there.

Two nicely completed loops. Good work, You.

The third placement option was with the domestic violence and rape crisis shelter. This experience would be brand new to me. I knew little of domestic violence (D.V.) or sexual violence apart from what I had read in books, watched in movies, or learned about in psych classes. My understanding was either fictionalized or academic. This was the beginning of a devastating loop I didn't know You would close later.

Just like I hadn't noticed the offices for the community mental health agency all those years I spent driving right by them, the D.V. shelter was another place I had driven by countless times without being aware of it. It was a normal-looking house, unidentifiable from the outside (as it should be), tucked along one of the most travelled roads. Awakening to the resources my hometown area had available made me wonder. How many other resources were offered in my community I hadn't known about growing up? Perhaps I hadn't had as open a mind as I thought and was *as* guilty of the very narrow mindedness I projected onto everyone else.

I hoped I would secure at least one placement. I never anticipated all three would offer me the chance to intern with them. After a grueling sophomore year—the death of my roommate, breaking up with my latest boyfriend (which turned into a month-long saga), being only one step ahead of depression—I couldn't wait to ignore the ghosts of September to May.

I accepted all three internships as my Accomplishment Identity could not possibly say no to any of them.

So excited at how amazing they would look on my application… Such feelings of being unstoppable, which I hadn't felt in months… Such hope that maybe, just maybe, I *could* change the world… This elation almost tempered the very real feelings about my own mortality…so much so I didn't recognize until I was in it, these were not *uplifting* places to be.

All three internships were a long hard look at reality. I faced the threat of fear and death every day through the people I worked with. I observed pain and suffering. I saw darkness. Darkness beyond what I had imagined. To me there couldn't have been a reality worse than young people dying, and then I saw so many other realities that, if not worse, were at least as horrible.

The elderly in the care of the geriatric facility were closer to death than any of us. On any day, I could show up for work only to be told one of my darlings had passed since I was last there. The adults I served in the Persistent Mental Health unit were often suicidal. Any day could be a day they chose to attempt their own end. The victims and survivors at the rape crisis shelter feared death if they stayed with their abusers, but felt it no less in their escape. Because what if her abuser found her?

While there was plenty to be wary of with the elderly and the mentally ill, the women in the shelter, the women using the hotline, were the ones who concerned me the most. Their battle was not with their own mind. Their battle was not with their aging body or disease. Their battle was with another person. A person who had claimed to love them. A person who had fathered their children. A person who had made desperate apologies, who had gone through intense periods of remorse after beating them, giving them the slightest hope he would change, before the cycle started all over again.

You could provide doctors and pills for the elderly. You could provide therapists, psychologists, and more pills for the mentally ill. While I'm not so naïve to think all these modalities always worked, there were at least multiple remedies to employ for their ailments and challenges. What did we have to offer the women at the Crisis Shelter?

Women who were hiding? Who were not always believed? Who had been cut off from other resources?

Certainly, doctors could help with cuts and broken bones. Nurses could help with rape kits. They could offer medications to allay pain or anxiety or bring sleep, but they couldn't treat the *actual* problem.

What was to be done about their abuser?

I would show up to the elder-care facility, and there was joy I had arrived. A smiling face come to spend time with them. My heart was always a little fuller upon leaving. The joy mutual. I enjoyed going.

I would work with the mentally ill, and though depressed or agitated, they were at least relieved to be heard and to have someone support them in their day-to-day functioning. My work with the rest of their case team was valuable, ensuring their needs were met and their quality of life was a little bit better while they navigated their diagnosis. That, too, brought a sense of fulfillment. I felt I was contributing, and my part mattered.

But nothing could describe the fear I felt, or the anxiety, on nights I wore the beeper and worked the hotline. I had a hard time falling asleep thinking, if I did, I would miss the desperate call of a woman in need. Instead, I'd lie awake, looking out the window, up at the moon, praying no one was at harm that night. Some nights praying worked. The following day, my eyes would burn with lack of sleep, but there was such relief I hadn't been called to the hospital. I drank more coffee and went about the rest of the day.

Then there were nights when the beeper startled me upright. My hands would sweat as I grabbed it to look at the number. My fingers would tremble as I called them—whoever 'they' were—completely unsure what I was about to receive, and what I might have to do.

One night, I was asked to go to the hospital. I tiptoed down the hall to my parents' room, my jeans and t-shirt already on, and knocked softly before opening the door slightly.

"I have to go to the hospital. I got a call," I whispered into their room.

"Be careful. Let us know when you're back," my mom said. Dad remained asleep next to her.

Off I went in the middle of the night. No one on the roads. The town so eerily dark and quiet. I turned on the radio to keep me sharp, alert, and my mind off how anxious I was.

Stepping inside the ER's sliding doors was jolting, those fluorescent lights blasting onto my face, forcing my body fully awake, though my mind was running sprints.

What was I walking into? Black eyes? Fat lips? Broken bones? Sexual assault?

Considering I was only in my twenties, the situation felt strange but powerful as I announced my presence at the ER nurse's station, letting them know I was there as an advocate. Me—still a baby, really—I had the ability to wake judges from their slumber, to request Temporary Relief from Abuse Orders when I needed them, because the forty hours of training I completed conferred on me that authority.

"Hi, I'm responding to a hotline call. I'm an advocate with Macy's House. I'm here to see Martha," I told the ER nurse, also giving her the name of the woman on the other side of the beeper number.

"Room nine. Down on the right," she said, hardly looking up at me and shuffling papers between clipboards.

I took my time walking to the right number on the wall, hearing my sneakers squeak on white tile floor. At room number nine, I knocked gently before I opened the door just enough to speak.

"Martha? This is Ally. We spoke on the phone a little bit ago. I'm responding to your hotline call."

"Come in," she says quietly.

I stepped into the room, drawing in a deep breath as I went.

The forty-something woman, with brittle, shoulder-length auburn hair, sat on a gurney with her hospital gown covering her. She started to cry, her shoulders moving up and down. She held on to fists full of the gown in her lap.

I gave her a moment and thought about what to say. I tried not to stare at the fresh red marks around her neck, or the bruise forming under her eye. Though I would need to note all of it for my report, and possibly for the relief of abuse order.

How could someone who is supposed to love you do that?

"I'm glad you called," I told her.

She sniffled and reached for a tissue at her bedside.

"Would you like to talk about what happened?" I asked.

"I can't go back there," she said, shaking her head, her eyes wide with terror.

My heart skipped.

Think. Think.

"Let's talk about some options then, okay?" I offered.

We chatted about some possibilities, but nothing I said felt right. Suddenly my training was completely lost on me. I called my coordinator to figure out whether we had space at the shelter, and to find out what I *should* be doing. We didn't have space at the shelter at that moment, so Martha called a friend to stay with for the night.

"But I need to go home and get a few things," she said "I hurried here without anything."

I did not like the sound of that.

It was the middle of the night. There weren't Ubers or Lyfts back then. There was hardly a taxi service in our area, and certainly not one operating at that hour, even though it had been how she got to the hospital in the first place. She was in no shape to walk from the hospital back to the place where she lived. And for whatever reason, there was no offer of transportation from her friend, who would let her crash on the couch.

The answer should have been, "Whatever it is. It can wait." The answer should have been, "We just need to get you where you need to go." The answer should have been, "I'm sorry, but I can't let that happen. It's against protocol."

Except I didn't say any of that.

I offered to drive her to her home. The place she shared with her abuser. And then to her friend's house.

While she finished up with the nurse, I called the judge and put in a request for a Temporary Relief of Abuse Order. Then, we walked out. I noticed she favored one leg a little more than the other.

We found my car. My legs shook getting into the driver side. The steering wheel occasionally slipped beneath my palms.

While we drove, she reassured me he wasn't there, and she would be fast. Clearly my nervousness was showing. I was supposed to be her advocate and protector, but here she was reassuring me, instead.

I parked alongside the curb across the street from the unlit house and turned my lights off. She scurried as fast she could across the road in the dark. I watched her, and I wondered if I had done the right thing. What if he was lurking on the other side of the lights? What would I do? How many minutes should I let her collect her stuff before I should go in after her? Or leave her? What if he came up behind my car and started banging on my window? With her gone, I realized how bad a plan I had laid out.

This was easily one of the dumbest and bravest things I've done. In equal measure. I'm sure You can agree.

I fidgeted in my seat and suddenly had the urge to pee. I couldn't stop looking out the windows, into the rearview mirror, and across the street.

Though I saw her coming back across with a duffle bag in tow, I still jumped when the door handle clicked and she got back into the car.

I chauffeured her to her friend's house—me, her (stupid) knight in shining armor. She squeezed my hand in thanks before she left, and I drove home, my heart beating so rapidly I felt it everywhere in my body. When I was back in my own house, I crept down the hall to my parents once more and re-announced my arrival.

"Everything OK?" mom whispered.

"Uh, yep."

In my room, I climbed into bed with my clothes on, looked up at the moon, and begged for no more calls that night. While there were still more calls to come that summer, that 'heroic midnight charade' went undetected and unknown, and there were no other harrowing tales of driving getaway wagons.

All summer I wondered how these women coped with their fear every day, because my fifteen minutes of sheer terror driving Martha that one night was enough to drive me to a panic attack. During the entire internship, I looked at these women with total awe.

Most of the women I connected with inside the shelter had children to consider. Add the intricacies of motherhood and protecting their young to the dynamics of power and abuse, and these women were warriors, with whole tales to tell and layers of scars (some visible, some not) to understand.

The mentally ill were warriors, too. Trying to slay the villains and monsters their hallucinations were made of. Fighting off their own thoughts, attempting to untangle reality from delusion, as though it might be possible to figure out which was which.

The elderly seemed to have lived a thousand lifetimes, going through such different childhoods, living in such different worlds than the one I navigated. They had just as much to say. They fought uphill battles, faced their own demons, overcame their own challenges.

Day after day, I asked questions, I listened, I observed, and I repeated back what I heard, to ensure I understood, but also to ensure they felt validated in their reality, their existence. I didn't know that was what I was doing, of course. I only knew to be kind, to be friendly, to be supportive. To be the best of what it means to be human.

In being allowed into their worlds—real or delusional, for it was all truth to them, regardless—my vantage point of humanity changed. I saw more darkness and suffering than that which comes from the death of a loved one. Despite that, my desire to make a difference remained. My compassion for people widened. My need to honor and share others' stories grew.

There was darkness, there was no denying it, but inside that darkness was also strength, bravery, truth, hope, and light.

In awe of suffering and strength,

Your well-intentioned advocate (and idiot)

QUESTIONS FOR YOUR PATH TO BRAVERY

From what lens do you see the world? How does it serve you on your own path?

What stories have you heard or borne witness to that have left a mark? Changed the way you see the world? Or the way you live your life?

Letter 13
THE OTHER SIDE OF THE WORLD

Dear Epic Pooper of Parties,

My interest in Australia dated back to the third grade when we were given pen pals who lived in Papua New Guinea. While the island has been independent from Australia since the 70s, I think my teachers likely simplified the geography for us by saying it was next to Australia, and so in my mind, it was a *part of* Australia. I can still picture the red, white, and blue striped lines around the edge of the envelopes that carried letters from my pen pal. Someday I would grow up and travel there—to Australia, that is.

The summer after Kaitlyn's death, and the same summer I zipped around from one internship to the other trying to save the world, I convinced my parents to let me do a semester abroad the following spring. My PowerPoint presentation was very convincing (as had my letter to my father been when I was nine and saw a black cat at the Humane Society in desperate need of rescue—Cocoa became a member of the family shortly after). Though it's also possible they wanted to offer me a change of scenery and a change of pace after staring death in the face only a few months prior.

They had asked me on more than one occasion if I wanted to take a semester off, or transfer. I didn't want to do either of those, but I did want to go to Australia. I did want the chance to travel, to see the other side of the world, before graduate school was upon me, and the rest of life happened.

I was so excited about flying across the globe, being in a new country, getting my passport stamped, meeting the locals. There was a decent amount of fear around the gigantic, poisonous snakes, and the variety of sharks, but I figured both were easy to avoid. I couldn't wait to be surrounded by the accent and the sun. To be on an adventure. To be a world-traveler at 20. To celebrate my 21st in a foreign country (not that becoming of U.S. drinking-age was going to matter overseas). How worldly I would become while there. And if I could brave going to the other side of the world all by myself—no adults I knew, no classmates who were coming, too—there was nothing else I couldn't do. That feeling of invincibility returned, even though I knew it was false.

Except Your ideas and my ideas about seeing the other side of the world were different. Really different. There are still some days I'm not sure how I ever forgave You.

My ideas were about culture, landscape, custom. Yours were about something else I still have trouble putting into words. I still can't decide if I think You *made* this happen for reasons I'll never know, or You merely *knew* it would happen, and then did Your best to guide me through it. (You know, ol' "Footprints" again.) Seriously, though, who decides up There what happens exactly? You or God? Do you flip a coin? Hold a conference call?

January 16, 2006. I always remember the 16, because it was eerie to me that 16 was the same date in September when Kaitlyn was pronounced dead. A year and four months later, and some part of me died, too, even though I continued to walk, talk, and breathe.

I had been on the Gold Coast for eleven days. I was out again with new girlfriends I had met in the airport. We had all arrived on the same plane and stood in line at customs to be stamped in. One was from New Jersey. One was from Wisconsin. I wasn't sure if I should claim Vermont or Ohio.

On the eleventh night, the three of us found ourselves yet again with the same group of guys we met the first day we were there. One of them, a tall, broad, and dark-haired guy from Brazil, rode from the airport to campus with us. He was the singular male in a bus of predominantly American girls. I watched as the girls around me talked over one another to get his attention and bat their eyes. Wisconsin was entranced. Brazil was polite and, also, suave. He was clearly used to this level of attention.

Every night since we had arrived, there were parties just for the abroad students before the local students returned to campus. Every night we found ourselves getting dressed up according to party theme, and failing to keep Wisconsin away from Brazil and the pack he traveled in—a group of multi-national guys who all attended university in the U.K., but who had not a single country in common among them. What they had in common were three things: their wealth (which they were happy to flaunt); their fashion (wearing trendy European styles and designer brands); and their language (they each spoke at least three).

While it seemed we were the most unlikely lot of girls to capture their interest, Wisconsin was so relentless in her pursuit, not only did we end up spending our first evening with them, but we tagged along with them from that moment on. Wisconsin was this cute, blonde cheerleader determined to make the Brazilian guy fall in love with her. To have some kind of semester abroad affair she could write home about, in the way you see YA romance novels play out. She had a girl-next-door naivety and a doe-eyed, giggly way about her. She also still had what the rest of us didn't: her virginity.

I was terrified for her.

For myself, I was sure my naivety had been wiped out, not only by Kaitlyn's death, but by my troubles with young love, and my new awareness of the darkness of humanity gifted to me by three summer internships. Not to mention how many times, in preparation for this trip, adults talked to me about drinking safely and about safety in numbers.

I watched Wisconsin. I watched her drink.

I never let myself get too tipsy.

I never let my own drink out of my hand. When I carried it, I carried it with my palm covering the top part of the glass.

I went in groups, everywhere I went.

I made note of my surroundings.

I was smart.

I was careful.

I was taking all the right precautions.

But I was also trusting, even while I was conscientious.

On that eleventh night, after a few drinks, I needed to use the restroom. There was no public bathroom in this bar located on the bottom floor of one of the dorm buildings. My only guess was they didn't feel the need to have a public restroom, since each room had its own.

"I need to use the bathroom. Will you come with me, once I find one?" I asked Wisconsin.

"Just ask Australia. He's got a room down the hall."

That was her way of declining.

"Hey, can I use your bathroom really quickly?" I asked Australia, another boy we had only just met.

"No, Mate. My room is a mess right now." Then he moved past me to go to the bar.

"You can use mine," said Denmark, Brazil's best friend. I hadn't realized he'd been paying attention to my conversation. "I've got a room up on the ninth."

The ninth floor felt like a good distance away, and I wasn't likely to get New Jersey to come along with me, any more than Wisconsin. I considered my alternatives.

I could walk across campus in the dark, by myself, to the first public restroom I could find, and then make my way back again alone.

Denmark tilted his head to look at my face. "It won't take long. You won't miss anything."

The safer and faster option seemed to just go with him up to the ninth floor. I would go. I would pee. I would return. It all could be done in five minutes.

I nodded and we walked to the elevator. It was the first time I had been alone with anyone since I arrived. We got into the elevator silently, the doors shutting out music, laughter, and the clinking of glasses. Sounds of a normal 20-something's existence.

"This a pretty nice building to live in for the semester," I said, stepping off the elevator, realizing the hallway looked far more like a ritzy hotel in comparison to the one in the building where I was staying.

"Yeah. My father secured my room well in advance."

I nodded.

We chatted down the hall, drawing from the handful of things we knew about each other. I didn't feel there was a reason for any significant pause. He wasn't a complete stranger, lurking in the bushes, never revealing his face. We had spent a week's worth of evenings together, watching from the sidelines as our friends did their tango. But you don't really know someone in eleven nights of drinking and small talk.

I walked into his room. The door shut.

From that moment, time went into slow motion. And in those long, long moments—that may have actually been only a few minutes in real time—I was reminded of this nightmare I used to have when I was four.

I know I must have been four, because my brother was in a crib, and we were sharing a room then. There was a single window. Straight ahead, fifty feet away from the house, was a pine tree. Behind it, a streetlamp propelled just enough light to cast a shadow around the tree and onto our front yard. I would often fall asleep at night staring out that window, though I wouldn't realize it until the terror of the nightmare thrust me awake.

I'd be staring out at that calming pine tree, then suddenly a Shadow Man appeared. He reminded me of those silhouettes you see decorating the sides of buildings—the cowboy with his leg kicked up, hat tilted down, leaning against the siding. Except this Shadow Man lurked. He crept. He had no hat. And he had no cowboy pistol. He brought with him a knife.

Shadow Man was silent. Shadow Man was slick.

He was able to lift my bedroom window with ease, without a sound, which was masterful, because during the day, the window creaked and moaned, desperate for oil. And at the end of the day, it was shut and locked.

Shadow Man was there only for me. He left my baby brother sleeping and unharmed.

Shadow Man climbed into my bed.

And he cut off my arms. Then my legs.

I never felt the removal of my limbs. There was no pain. I never saw blood. I only felt suddenly they weren't there. Like that feeling after you've lain on your arm too long and cut off the circulation.

Shadow Man rendered me silent. Even though I could still feel my tongue, I could make no sound. While I could feel my mouth stretch open to scream, though his hands never covered my mouth, nothing came out but dried whispers, "Help." Though by then, the damage was done, that was the point when I always woke up, never having realized I had fallen asleep.

Still feeling the presence of the Shadow Man somewhere near, I would jump out of bed, scurry across the hall, violently attack my mother's shoulder, and she would lift the comforter without any words and allow me entry to her bed. I'd fall asleep with my feet shoved underneath her thighs, cool fresh sweat dampening my cotton nightgown.

That nightmare had been frequent until I moved out of that room. Perhaps because I could no longer stare out the window at that tree. What was strange was, the dream came to me once a year after that, until adulthood. A mysterious haunting I couldn't explain. Why did it start to begin with? Why did it come every year? What did it mean?

Were You trying to tell me something?

There I was, on my back, my skirt and underwear pulled off, him on

114

top of me…and I couldn't feel my body. My arms. My legs. I couldn't scream, though my mouth was open, and my tongue was very much there. He either couldn't hear, or chose to ignore my dryly whispered "No! No!"

I was immobile and inaudible.

No words. No voice. No power.

Until it was over.

I didn't learn until much later that "freeze" is also a response. For years I blamed myself for not having the fight-or-flight response, and instead "just lay there," when I should have tried harder. When I should have saved myself.

Then my voice returned. My ability to move returned. I slid off the bed, grabbed my underwear and skirt to redress, and I felt quiet tears run down my cheeks. My legs wobbled as I stepped back into my underwear, my fingers shook as I rebuttoned my denim skirt. I know exactly what I was wearing. Can still see myself in that skirt and the tank top I had on. I never wore them again.

Every time I blinked back tears to right my vision, all around were darkness and shadows. Had the sun gone down after I entered the room, or had it already been dark outside?

He stood watching me, waiting for something. He was talking, but I couldn't hear him.

Some part of me was now far, far away.

My body moved quickly once I was dressed, or at least I assumed it must have. I found myself in front of the elevator feverishly hitting the button to go back down.

Where was I going? My mother was so far away.

I'd come to Australia to see another part of the world. To forget about the inevitability and unpredictability of death. To forget about pain and suffering. To live. To laugh. To revel. To travel. I tried desperately to hold onto those things still. The reasons I went there. And I tried desperately to understand what happened that night. And why. To figure out if I had walked right into the very den I'd been so adamant about protecting Wisconsin from entering.

I blamed myself. I felt ashamed I had let it happen. There were even times I wondered if I had consented somehow, but couldn't remember. I told almost no one. Only mentioned it in passing to a couple of friends, dropping 'the bomb,' closing the conversation, and then moving on. They never asked anything more. I tried to explain it to Wisconsin in an effort to protect her, but it did no good. I told my boyfriend, the only person I tried to keep the conversation open with, but he closed it down, choosing denial and suppression for the preservation of our long-distance relationship. Keeping it hidden was the way forward, especially from my mom or dad.

Since I had convinced my parents to let me come, since they had spent additional money to send me, since I had told myself from the age of eight I would do this, I would not jeopardize the rest of my semester. So, I remained. I stayed until May. It was the longest three months I've ever experienced which turned into the longest three years and impacted every relationship for the next decade.

I made some new friends. I saw some new places. I took a lot of pictures. I walked past my rapist almost daily. On at least two occasions, we had words. Once in a conversation, when I attempted to understand what happened. Once at a semi-formal, when I found Wisconsin had slipped away from our girl group to drink with them at their table, and I begged her to leave with us. Both times, he called me a liar and a slut, and he told me I wasn't welcome, and to leave.

Mostly, I worked out. I stayed in my room. I stayed away from parties. I pulled away from that first group and found a new one. I emailed my boyfriend back home. And I maxed out calling cards.

This was not the adventure I had in mind.

How come that had to happen? Was my childhood dream an omen You sent and I failed to heed? Was my hotline advocacy and internship at the shelter preparation?

Kay is now four, and he has nightmares. When he calls out, panicked, in the middle of the night, or finds his way into my room, I have a difficult time ushering him back into his bed. What if he has his own version of the Shadow Man there waiting for him? And I've tucked him back in, because parenting books and blogs tell me co-sleeping isn't healthy, and it's a terrible habit to break.

I used to be that child with the nightmare. Then I was the young adult *in* the nightmare. Now I'm a parent. A parent who knows I can't always protect my young—which is an entirely different nightmare I can't fathom. I won't always be just across the hall. I won't always be able to tell the good guys from the bad ones. The only thing I can do is hope he never sees that nightmare part of the world, and if he does, he's brave enough to face it. That he's brave enough to tell me.

Still pretty pissed at you,

The jaded world traveler

QUESTIONS FOR YOUR PATH TO BRAVERY

What's a personal injustice you've lived through? How did it
strengthen and shape you?

What would help you release a past trauma or pain?

Letter 14
STEPPING INTO THE LIGHT

Dear Spiritual Guide,

You gave me a serious gift when you gave me the opportunity to teach Introduction to Women's Studies. At first it just seemed like the answer to my financial prayers, but it turned into being *so much more* than just paying the tuition bill and making my master's degree possible. I didn't even know women's studies was an academic study at the time I interviewed for it. But just as I had clinched the deals on my internships back in undergrad, I nabbed the assistantship. There was only one spot. Only one opportunity for one master's student, and it was given to me. You knew I needed so desperately what it had to offer.

Women's studies was my first formal academic education in the *isms* (racism, sexism), institutional oppression, pro-life versus pro-choice, the wage gap, and matters of the LGBTQ community—among other things. Of course, some of these things had presented themselves along the way (on the playground, in the school hallways, on the college campus), but never had I ever been given the ideology or the language. Me, the words girl, had been without a whole vocabulary or paradigm. Finally, so many things now could be described, explained, or even understood.

It was the first time I learned the word *feminist* and proudly claimed

119

it. The first time I cared about politics and my right to vote. The first time I ever heard the idea 'the personal is political,' and understood how women's experience connected us, and why it is important to our liberation. The first time I started to recognize parts of myself. Parts of myself that weren't necessarily connected to writing or dreaming. The parts of myself that cared about people, justice, advocacy—humanity. The world at large.

I started to see my younger self in a different way. To understand my experiences via a different lens. To examine my femininity, my gender, my sexuality, and the experiences that intersected with those elements of my person. The world where all of this exists was one I had never seen before. It was both cruel and beautiful. Just and unjust. Liberating and oppressive. Finally, I had a whole picture, where both darkness and light existed.

As I was steeped in this new perspective and way of thinking, I was introduced to thought-leaders and movement-makers and paradigm-shakers I had never known before. I was also introduced to powerful women writers and change agents. Names like Gloria Steinem, Bell Hooks, Audre Lorde, Lilly Ledbetter, and Eve Ensler were now in my canon. It was Ensler's work that personally empowered and impacted me the most.

Her famous *The Vagina Monologues* (her award-winning play) and V-Day (the global activist movement to end violence against women and girls) moved me from silently-suffering-sexual-assault-victim to strong-and-unashamed-sexual-assault-survivor. She was essential to the integration of my victim-self and my survivor-self, though I didn't realize it until the moment it happened.

When I agreed to co-direct the local V-Day fundraiser presentation through our Women's Studies Department, I was focused on the primary cause: raising money for the local rape crisis shelter. It was fundraising and advocacy and changemaking at its core, and it was safe. I could fight the fight and make my stance by putting on a good show, without having to claim my own experience.

No one had reason to tell me—and I had no reason to ask—about what routinely happened at the end of the performance. I probably could have watched the whole show on the Internet somewhere and caught this final segment and therefore been made aware, but I didn't.

I knew all I thought I needed to know to direct an awesome fundraiser. That part was true; I was prepared for an awesome fundraiser. Kendra (my co-organizer) and I had done great work.

But I wasn't prepared as a victim.

What I hadn't known going into it was, after the last monologue was read, someone would come forward to provide a couple of sentences about the V-Day mission. In this case, it was the director of our department, Pam.

The lights started to come up a little in the house, the spotlight no longer just on the stage. With more light, you could see the small theater was packed. It probably didn't fit more than 100 people, and we had sold out every seat. It was "standing room only." People in the back along the wall. People along the side, leaning in the aisle. I remember the blood-orange carpet running down the aisles, the brown-cushioned theater seats—a sign of the 70s, I guessed. There were dings and scratch marks on the walls and on the arm rests between seats.

Pam gave the spiel about the purpose for our fundraiser. Made sense.

But then…

Then she asked all those in the room who had survived sexual violence to stand and be recognized for their strength and resilience.

Every single inch of my body came to life with goosebumps.

The hair on the back of my neck stood up. My throat engorged as though I were having an allergic reaction. My eyes filled.

People all around me started to rise from their seats.

And not just a few.

A lot.

The squeaking of old and unoiled seats as they retracted on themselves took my breath away.

That 1-in-4 statistic (the reality that one in four women would be raped in her lifetime), I never forgot after I learned it was more like one in two inside the theater.

Could there actually be that many of us right there in the room?

I watched two of my colleagues move away from the walls they were leaning on to stand firmly in the center of their aisle. The same devastated look across their faces I imagined mine, too, held in that moment. Others wobbled to their feet, holding tightly to the hand of the person seated next to them.

With the feeling that my throat was coated with chalk, and my heart had somehow managed to find its way outside of my chest—pounding so heavily I thought the person on the end of the row next to me might be able to hear it—I, too, slid, shaky-kneed away from the wall into an upright position, daring myself to be seen in the upturned house lights.

Every part of me shook. Even my face, as though my body were seizing. The Rape did not want to be recognized. It shrieked inside as though it were a fierce witch, and I was dousing it with water.

I held my hands together in front of me so tightly my knuckles hurt, but I hoped it would steady me. I hoped it would ease the knot in my throat that was blocking my windpipe.

It was the first time I ever stood as a victim.

It was the first time I made a public acknowledgement of my assault.

It was the first time I didn't feel alone.

It was the first step I made toward becoming a survivor.

In the next moment, Pam asked the people who knew a survivor to stand. More bodies rose to mount their feet to the floor. Lastly, those people who were committed to standing with us, to stop sexual violence against women, were also asked to rise. Every single remaining person rose to their feet. A room of over 100, standing tall and straight. The magnitude of it was so powerful, it unlocked a sound trapped inside my chest, and a small whimper trembled off my lips.

I can't say that being seen was immediately easy or comfortable after that, but it was better than being alone or being silent.

The following year, the stakes rose.

Kendra and I were determined to blast by our fundraising tally from the year before. We were in a space with a much greater seating capacity and a bigger stage. We had way more tickets to sell, and we were doing more than one show. Beyond that, my mom, my sister, and Lonnie would be attending. They were flying out to Ohio to watch the play and rise to their feet when it was time. Just months before the second fundraiser (but three years after my assault), I had finally shared what happened in Australia. Finally, released my secret. Finally, I was trying to fit together the pieces of the me before and the me after, so I could feel whole again.

While this time I knew what happened at the end of the performance, there was no predicting how I would feel this second time, with my family just a few feet away. Last year I had blindly stepped into the light, not knowing I would. Not knowing I would have the option. And mostly, I stepped up in front of strangers.

This second year, my assault was more real to me, less abstract, even though it was further away in time. I was now 'out' about what had happened. I was now visible to my friends and family in ways I hadn't been. It made it harder in some ways because it required I be more vulnerable.

When Pam stepped out onto stage signaling it was nearly time, my body started to quake. Those words again came over the speaker:

"I ask that all those in the room who have survived sexual violence stand and be recognized for their strength and courage."

In my periphery, I could see my mom and sister and Lonnie watching, waiting. They were here to bear witness to my pain. My vulnerability. This time, instead of choking back sounds, I wept.

"I invite those in the room who know a survivor, to stand and join them."

Kendra came to my side and grabbed my hand. I watched tears roll down her cheeks as she looked me in the eyes, holding space for my pain, honoring my experience. And then I looked past her and saw my family rise to their feet. My sister's eyes glistened with tears, and she hugged her arms to her chest. Lonnie reached for tissues in her pocket. My mom with her fingertips pressed to her lips, swayed ever so slightly from side to side. The way I imagine she did when I was a baby. When she thought she could protect me from the world.

"Lastly," Pam said, "For anyone committed to standing with us to stop sexual violence against women, we invite you to rise."

The sound of folding chairs scratching across concrete echoed in the space.

"Let's take a moment of silence to honor those who have not survived at the hands of violence," Pam said.

When the silence was over, one by one, the actresses came on stage to hold hands and bow. Over the speakers came Whitney Houston's "I Wanna Dance with Somebody." I made my way over to my family. I hugged Lonnie. I hugged my sister. I stepped into my mother, and she enclosed me in her arms.

"I hope you can start to feel a little better now."

Then she swayed to the music and sang the lyrics softly in my ear, as I rested my head on her shoulder.

Over time, as distance from the assault has grown, as understanding and a new perspective of that singular traumatic event has evolved, and as shame has disappeared from my emotional reference, I have found, when the time has been right or appropriate for sharing openly, deeply, and honestly about my assault, it has brought deep connection and mutual vulnerability. Humanity needs more vulnerability and more connection. We need women to know they're not alone. Not to suffer silently.

We need our Eve Enslers. We need the women to write about suffering—theirs and others. We need women (and men) to spearhead movements and demand systems change. We need to educate people about violence and consent and sexism and oppression and the great many other isms that contribute to hate and power used as a weapon. We need those of us brave enough to be recognized to step into the light, and to open space for others to bravely follow.

Thank You for bringing me to the light,

A surviving member of 1-in-4

QUESTIONS FOR YOUR PATH TO BRAVERY

How do you honor the difficult parts of your journey? How can you integrate them with your life?

What does vulnerability look like to you? How do you believe it might serve you?

Letter 15
CHOOSING WRITING—ACT TWO

Dear Pointer of Paths,

In claiming feminism, in finding a tribe, I started to feel more aligned with myself. I'm not sure I would have called it *alignment* then. Likely not. But that's what it was. For the first time in a long time I remembered who I was all those years ago, barefoot in the woods—a time of childhood before dreams were encouraged away, hearts were broken, people died, and parts of yourself were stolen. In *alignment* came strength. A will and determination to take charge of what I wanted.

As such, I performed an act of beautiful and selfish bravery. For the first time since the day in my bedroom when I adamantly chose Bread Loaf over prom, I chose writing. I chose the pursuit of that dream.

There I was, well into my second semester in the Marriage and Family Therapy (MFT) master's program, which I selected when I couldn't reason crippling myself in financial debt by attending the Doctor of Psychology (Psy.D.) program I'd been admitted to. It had hurt a little to decline the seat there, after working so hard to ensure I would get a place in a doctorate-level program. But I couldn't take the chance at being that much in debt for the rest of my life.

This MFT program was attractive, though, as it offered the

possibility of an assistantship (which I got) and was far less expensive to begin with. Plus, it still pointed me in the direction of becoming a psychologist. (Ok, and I got to stay in Ohio, close to the guy I was in love with at the time, which was a bonus. Not that *that* worked out... thank God—and You, of course—that it didn't.)

My life was going according to plan. All the little boxes checked off. But I wasn't happy. Not even close. I sat in classes and I couldn't stop daydreaming. The last time my mind had wandered that frequently was elementary school, when I was working on a book project I couldn't wait to race home to finish.

Here I was in my mid-twenties, sitting in a Theories class, coming up with fictional backstory and narrative for two of my professors: identical twins who both taught in the program. In actual fact, they lived together and were rumored to have never been married, and to have done everything together since birth (including going to the same schools, getting the same degrees, and now teaching in the same program). They were ripe for a good story. I couldn't help myself.

Their tales for me started off just as doodles within the margins of my notebook. Short sentences, phrases. Soon, I was filling up full college-lined notebook papers with stories about them, instead of taking actual notes. I found myself sitting in the back of the class, week after week, further away from the podium or screen. I couldn't answer any of my classmate's questions about upcoming assignments. I became more and more disinterested and distracted. I nearly stopped listening altogether.

The burning need to write was there in full force, reminding me of the afternoons and evenings as a child in my bedroom, or at the family computer, lost in my own worlds and words. The fevered strokes of my pen, scrolling silly stories about The Twins, were as though a great beast that was hibernating had awakened, and now it was hungry. It needed to be fed.

It was exhilarating.

What about all I had worked for? What about all the people I had told I was going to be a psychologist? What about all those internships I had worked? All the people I had helped? What did it all mean, if I just walked away?

And what would I walk toward? I had become so comfortable planning, creating checklists, and following the right order of operations, a part of me was terrified not knowing what it all meant. But another part of my spirit rejoiced in the possibilities that came with taking a new direction.

I looked into what other disciplines the university offered for Master's.

(I have to imagine this is where You come in. Or perhaps You came in earlier, when you dissuaded me from the PsyD. program and sent me in this direction, knowing …)

The university had just started a Master of Fine Arts program in creative writing…

My prayers were answered! The path was made clear.

I wouldn't have to leave my assistantship, which I loved.

I wouldn't have to walk away from tuition reimbursement, which I needed.

I wouldn't have to leave Ohio, not yet, still hopeful of this (stupid) boy's love returning.

I wouldn't have to quit getting a Master's degree, or take any longer to attain it.

I just needed to switch.

Oh, but the fear and the threat of regret in losing all that I had worked for. The requirement to face my parents, to tell them I was giving up on this part of the plan so I could pursue a dream that had lived inside me since the days I made up stories in the trees.

How would I tell them that? What would they say?

Would I shrink back into those check boxes that were still there, telling me to stay the course. Psychology was my direction. Do not turn back now.

I just couldn't bear it.

The longer I showed up for my therapy classes, the more I resented them. The more I wrote in the margins of my notes. The more my instincts were solidified. I was not in the right place.

With careful vetting to ensure I could make a smooth program transition, I made *the* phone call. (You know the one.)

My parents knew I was unhappy in my program, so this couldn't be a total shock to them, right?

My dad picked up.

We walked through our normal catch-up. I kept my responses short, on edge at the thought of telling him my decision, nerves constricting my intestines, squeezing them like a snake.

"I've made a decision."

"About what?"

"About my program. I'm still going to get my Master's, but not in marriage and family therapy."

There was a pause, but I could sense his head nodding.

"Are you thinking of coming home?"

I paused.

"No. I still want to get my Master's here, but I'm going to get it in creative writing."

Big inhale of air, and I held my breath.

Another pause, which gave me the chance to go into a long-winded and fast-paced explanation of all the details of the M.F.A. program, including the very practical considerations— such as, it wouldn't take me any longer to complete, I could start right away, my assistantship and tuition reimbursement would transfer, etc. (If only I had prepared another handy PowerPoint. I could have emailed it.)

"I see that you've done a lot of research and really understand how this would all work."

I bit my bottom lip.

Please don't say 'no,' whispered that little voice in my head, still begging for validation, and for permission from my parents for me to be a writer.

"But what are you going to do with it?"

"Do with what?" I tried desperately not to let adolescent attitude creep into my tone, but I was instantly back in my bedroom choosing Bread Loaf over prom.

"What are you going to do with an M.F.A? What are the job possibilities? How are you going to pay the bills as a writer?"

I hadn't known how to combat this question when I was a teen, and I didn't know how to combat this same question as an adult. But I knew it was what I had to do. This was what I wanted to be.

Before knowing exactly what I should say, I blurted out:

"Honestly, I have no idea."

After a brief pause, and before he could interject, I added:

"But I don't know how to fail. When I put my mind to something, I do it. I need you to trust me that I'll figure it out. That somehow, I'll make money and be able to pay my bills and take care of myself. This is what I want to do. And I'm going to do it."

Not, *I'm thinking about doing it*. Or, *I want to do it*. Or, *Will you let me do it?*

I'm doing it.

An affirmative action.

A going forward.

A claiming of what's mine.

A rejection of the check boxes.

A letting go and parting of ways with what I had worked for, to make space for what I wanted.

A big 'eff you' to following other's rules or simply accepting only one path.

A true listening to my intuition and self-guidance system.

A step closer to a life-long dream come true.

An act of bravery.

There is no harder feat than to be ourselves in the face of all the noise, all the expectation, all the standards that have been created out of everyone before us doing things one certain way.

In that moment, I chose me. I chose my dreams. I chose to believe in what a power so much bigger than myself was trying to tell me.

What YOU were trying to tell me.

That flicker, that flame, that light burning brightly and warmly inside me, telling me to follow it—it was powerful. It was guiding. It was truth.

I wanted it never to leave.

With pride in choosing me and my path,

Pursuer of dreams

QUESTIONS FOR YOUR PATH TO BRAVERY

If you created your own path which defied or released others' rules, what would it look like?

Where would your path lead? What would you pursue?

Letter 16
SIDE STEPS AND SIDE HUSTLES

Dear Purveyor of Lessons,

I regret, after getting my M.F.A. and putting in all that energy and effort to push forward passionately toward a writing career, my return to Vermont meant writing had to take another backseat. There were limited well-paid writing opportunities in VT (as far as I knew, then). But regardless, I moved back home. The young man I was with at the time wanted to live there and settle down.

I was done with Ohio by the time I completed my Master's. I missed my family, and the thought of being back somewhere comfortable and familiar, alongside the feeling this guy might just be *the one*, all seemed like pretty good reasons to return home and make the most of it. Even if writing would be *on the side,* the way my parents always told me it should be. (And it wasn't long before I began thinking they were right, but hell if I would ever say it out loud.)

The first job I got was with a non-profit. The mission was great. I was good at it. People liked me. But within a year, I was unhappy. Unfulfilled. I started looking again at writing options. I tried doing a little freelancing online, writing blog posts, but it didn't produce results. I started working on a children's book that came to me while I commuted all over the state for work. I joined a local writing organization that became my one consistent attachment to a writing life, and I got super involved there. You know, because that's what I always do. Or always did. (We both know, I'm still working on this.)

I kept searching for an opportunity that would let me be among words daily for my 9–5 and still pay the bills. There had to be some way. Finally, I saw my chance. An advertisement in one of the local papers for a job within an academic publishing company that just so happened to have an office located one town over from our apartment.

I was determined to get in there. I could feel it—that all-knowing feeling, like however-many-times before. I was right.

For the next three years, I had this period of satisfaction. I got to go to a job every day that I loved. I got to work with words, and books. I was with people I enjoyed. I was in a part of the state that I loved. I wrote my own stuff on my lunch breaks.

Also, during those three years, I got engaged, we bought a house with a fence and a yard and trees. We got a cat. We got married. Then we got a dog. Then I got pregnant.

The whirlwind of life events meant my own writing only ever happened a little bit here, a little bit there. But I felt comfortable with that, because my day job fulfilled that part of myself. Heading into my third year, I had the opportunity to move from the marketing department to the editorial department. Finally, I really felt like I had made it. I absolutely loved that job. But, You know, "all good things…" (Did You come up with that, or is it a Big Guy-ism?)

One day in July, my belly round, my feet swollen, we were all packed into the conference room at work, sun beating in, everyone sweating, and were told via video conference our company had been bought by another company. Our future was unknown.

The energy in the office immediately shifted; no one believed in a positive outcome. Everyone thought we should all start looking for other employment.

Other employment? At six months pregnant?

Other employment?

Where else would I get a job writing and working with books that paid actual money? This had been a miracle to begin with.

I decided I needed to wait until we all knew for certain what would happen to the company, to our office.

That day came in September. They dragged us back into the conference room. My belly was even bigger, and my son was kicking me up in my ribs. I waddled in and took a seat at the back, with space to sit thighs out. I was wearing these same ugly, black, slip-on shoes with every outfit, because my feet were two sizes bigger than usual, and they were the only flats I could find that fit. (Luckily, because of the size of my stomach, I usually couldn't see them, but they embarrassed me just the same.)

The company had sent The Suit this time. We had seen him several times since July, as he met with each department and department head, under the pretense he and the acquiring company were learning all they could, so they could most successfully merge the two companies. We all wanted to be cautiously optimistic, but most of us felt the end was near. Even still, when he delivered the news, we were as stunned as though we'd had no idea it was coming.

"We'll be closing the Burlington office," The Suit said.

I bit down on my lower lip and tried not to bolt immediately to go find a corner somewhere and fall apart. Except, The Suit had a lot more to say. Dates, timelines, technicalities. I tried to focus, but I was panicked. Here I was going on eight months pregnant, and I was being laid off.

Thanks, Universe. (The Epic Pooper of Parties strikes again.)

But I get it. That publishing house wasn't it. As awesome as it seemed, that isn't where You wanted me to be.

My last planned day in the office was bumped right up against my due date. I was due on a Monday, and my last day was the Friday two days before. Because You really do have a wild sense of humor—and for all I know, you teamed up with Kay in the womb, somehow—my first contraction was in the early hours Friday morning. I didn't go to work. That was the end of my publishing career.

I went on maternity leave, and I spent precious moments with Kay, begrudgingly applying for jobs in between breast feeding and the rest of infant care, in order to collect unemployment. While totally in love with my son, I grieved the loss of this job. I had lost my one connection to the part of myself that felt the most genuine. Writing would once again become a side hustle. A hobby. A dream I might get around to pursuing *some day.* (But when? After Kay went to college?)

I pitched the idea to my then-husband about staying at home. Figuring out how to write from home, to make some money somehow, and save on daycare costs. I had no interest in going back to work for some job I didn't care about, or having Kay in the care of someone we hardly knew. My husband at the time didn't think we could make it work. Trusting his calculations and understanding of our finances way better than I trusted my own, I resigned myself to finding a job that would work. It was my responsibility to bring in additional income to help my family.

Eventually, I got in at a law firm, with the pitch that my marketing skills, along with strong administrative skills, would lend themselves well to what they needed. Unfortunately, it was a terrible fit from the start, even though we all tried our best.

Well into the months that followed, I just couldn't shake the emptiness and unfulfillment returning. Added to that heap was such guilt I couldn't just appreciate the salary I brought into our family.

I wasn't even there a year before I started looking at other job opportunities. I even signed up for an online copywriting program, thinking I could finally figure out how to write from home and make money, if I could just finish this program and get the certificate. But wife, new mom, full-time career woman—there was so little time to devote to learning a new skill.

The one gift the law job offered me—I'm now certain You left it as a breadcrumb—was my first real itch to be an entrepreneur. Because the firm focused on working with entrepreneurs. Every day I learned about new Vermonters who were starting their own businesses and going out on their own. It was completely cool, and I found myself daydreaming about working for myself in addition to daydreaming about writing. What could that look like?

I kept my feet on solid ground, too, and shopped my resume and cover letter. A connection got me in at a rising company just around the corner. There was bright promise of upward movement, amazing benefits, and a great starting salary. That connection came through someone I had worked with at the publishing company. A sign? I thought so. But You tell me.

That was where You wanted me to go next. It had nothing to do with writing, but maybe, just maybe, this time the pay, the benefits, the possible upward advancement, would give me a sense of satisfaction. Maybe this time I could lean into what I was providing for my family and be happy.

For a little while, it worked. I had the chance to earn more than I could ever have imagined at any of my other jobs. I had the ability to be the spouse with better benefits, and we put everyone under my plan. I had the chance to make a name for myself in a new company, determined to go places. These felt like achievements to be proud of. Accomplishments others would be proud of, and things that would sound important when I talked to other professionals about 'what I do.'

Writing could stay a side hustle a little longer, right? It wasn't going anywhere…

Little did I know this job was the last stop. You were close to rounding out this journey. You were nearly through with the lessons You needed to dish out before I finally got it: *No one puts Writing in the corner.*

Hadn't I been hearing its call? Hadn't I been feeling how desperately it wanted to be a main character in my life?

It didn't want to be ignored any longer. Truthfully, neither did You. You had been attempting at every corner to lead me. Guide me. Show me. Teach me. What I was to do, what I was to be, was right there. I'm sorry I couldn't seize it faster.

With deepest apologies for being so dense,

Your kinda slow learner

QUESTIONS FOR YOUR PATH TO BRAVERY

What lessons do you believe the Universe has been trying to
teach you repeatedly?

If you finally understand them, how are you leveraging them?

If you've been ignoring them, why?

Letter 17
BECOMING A MOM

Dear Universe,

I know I've written You about a lot of dark times, but there's no denying my greatest joy in adulthood has been becoming a mom. Truly my greatest gift is Kay. (Okay, that and life. That I have air in my lungs and more days to exist.)

As soon as I knew I was pregnant, I began talking to him. While walking the dog, I would share with him what I hoped for him in life, how I hoped I would be as a mom, and what I was worried about. Specifically, I apologized in advance if I was crabby in the middle of the night or early mornings. I also apologized if there ever came a day when I wasn't there to protect him, but I promised I would do my absolute best, no matter what.

Pregnancy and delivery showed me how capable my physical body was. That, in and of itself, was miraculous to me. I still have no words to truly express how strong triumphing over labor and delivery made me feel. Like, if I could do *that*. I could do anything.

His entering into the world made me realize how deeply my heart could feel. How complicated and complex emotions could become. How every decision could be now reconsidered through the lens of caring for this little person. Or how all the conclusions I had previously come to about my childhood and my parents would turn on their head.

Becoming a mom has been this all-consuming experience, but it has been so fueling, so filling, so fun. Witnessing him interact with the world is now my favorite pastime. I relish our time together. I soak in every smile, every giggle, every reach for my hand, every spontaneous "I love you."

He's still small enough to want me close, to want to cuddle, to want to hold my hand as he falls asleep. He wants to play with me and be at my side, whether it's building a fort or helping cook dinner. When we get home, he wants to have dance parties. On weekends, he wants to make pancakes. For dinner he wants to make green eggs and ham, just like the book, which is one of his favorites (at least right now). He loves to read, which melts my heart.

More recently, he's started dictating his own stories and illustrations to make his own books. This makes every part of my insides soar. Sometimes he tells me when he grows up, he'll grow up to be a girl, "So I can be like you," he tells me. He doesn't realize yet, he'll turn out like me in some fashion, no matter what. We all end up like our parents to some extent.

Becoming a mom made me stop and check myself. More than all else, I wanted for him to grow up being true to himself and believing in his own dreams. Quickly, I realized in order for him to learn that, he would need to see it modeled. It was up to me to show him the way. That's what parenting is at the core, right? Not just feeding and clothing and basic needs, but ensuring their success when they're old enough to leave the nest. Giving them footholds. I want him to believe he can go wherever his heart (or You, as it were) might lead him.

Without Kay, I'm not sure how much longer it would have taken me to realize I needed to show up for myself. To truly consider what

I wanted for my life and who I wanted to be, and do it, already. You blessed me with Kay. In becoming a mom, I went searching to become myself. I went looking for ways to grab the moon, so I could show him how to lasso his own. Becoming a mom was entering a new land, a new landscape. One where my dreams and his could exist, if I dared enough to walk toward them and could brave whatever came my way in their pursuit. With Kay's life and future in my own hands, our shared blood running in each our veins, there was no choice. I had to choose *me* to choose him, too.

With undefinable amounts of thanks for making me a mother,

Kay's mom

QUESTIONS FOR YOUR PATH TO BRAVERY

What motivates or drives you to want to change the way you show up in your life?

If there were no limitations, restrictions, or barriers, what would you want for yourself and for your life?

Letter 18
I GAVE THEM A NAME

Dear Universe,

I still don't know how to address the greatest loss of my life—my blessed little one, my second baby. And I'm not a stranger to loss. Sophia was lost to illness. Kaitlyn lost to unexplainable, unexpected circumstances. My sense of control and safety lost to rape. I thought I knew what a hole in the heart felt like. I thought I already knew how badly pain could feel.

But the loss of a child? No. Nothing compares.

I was nine weeks along when my baby left my body. Eight when the first warning signs appeared. For eight weeks, I was in that early first trimester excitement. I still couldn't believe how quickly I got pregnant. Faster than with Kay. And I was elated the news was just in time for the Christmas holiday, creating wonderful opportunities for fun announcements to the grandparents—the only people we were telling that early on. We had waited the full first trimester with Kay before we uttered any word to anyone. But with this second pregnancy, I was in a rush to share. I remember saying to my then-husband, "Well, if something goes wrong, I'd rather have the support, knowing they know, than it being the first time they find out."

I had no reason to believe this second pregnancy would be any different than my first—which was full term and healthy the entire time. What made me decide this time I needed my parents, or his, to know early on, just in case? Was this the same knowing I had about being a writer? About going to that college? About getting that assistantship? Was it possible for me to understand, on some subconscious level, this pregnancy would not keep?

I was delighted at that first ultrasound, hearing that strong heartbeat and seeing my little bean on the screen. Ultrasounds had been my favorite part of my pregnancy with Kay. Especially early on, before I could feel him inside. They were like putting the call through to the other side and getting a response. For those few minutes, that little person I spent time talking to, I could now hear instead. That first ultrasound for this second child put the due date in August, and while it was a long way off, and the next ultrasound was, too, I had those pictures and the memory of the heartbeat to let me know everything was okay. I stared at those ultrasound pictures all the way home from the hospital and rubbed my thumb over them.

Then one Saturday, just wrapping up week eight, as I attended a day-long writing conference, I felt the slightest little push of moisture leave the space between my legs.

I sat listening to the second speaker. I knew that feeling. That feeling of just beginning my period. My throat tightened. I squeezed my legs together, willing whatever was happening to stop, and reminding myself there was no need to jump to conclusions. Being that I was emceeing the event, there were few opportunities to get to the bathroom, and truthfully, I was avoiding it. I didn't want to know. I didn't want to see.

At the end of the day, there was no avoiding it. I had been drinking coffee, tea, and water all day. I had to drive home. I needed to use the bathroom first. Just before grabbing my coat and heading for the car,

I stepped into the women's bathroom. Slid into a stall. Took a deep breath, and pulled my pants down.

Blood. On the one hand, it wasn't a lot. More like a light spotting the week before a period. Spotting could be normal during a pregnancy, right? Yet I had never spotted with Kay.

Do not panic. Do not jump to conclusions. I reminded myself and blinked back tears.

The ride home felt so long.

I had no sooner set foot in the kitchen, when I said, "I'm bleeding."

Silence.

We stared at each other.

Moments later, I called the Midwifery unit at the hospital. They said to monitor and, if it didn't get better or it got worse, to consider a trip to the ER where they could do a scan.

"Okay," I said and hung up.

I don't remember if we waited, or went to the ER right off, or if we went the next morning, but we went. We spent hours in the waiting room before we were brought to a room. And then several more hours.

The outcome was our baby had 50% viability. The baby might make it or not, but there was nothing for us to do. There was nothing I could do to ensure the baby's safety. There was nothing I could do to prevent the bleeding. For the second time in my life, I had no control of my body. Except this time, this time, the assailant was inside me and was attacking my baby.

I was sent home to watch and wait. I would return in one week for another scan to see what was going on.

For an entire week, I watched more blood leave my body. For an entire week, I cried every time I went to the bathroom and every time I came back out—reporting I was still bleeding. For an entire week I prayed, *Please don't take my baby.* For an entire week, I tried to focus my attention, and any joy I could muster, on Kay. My mother came and sat with me, to watch movies and to talk, to pass the time, and watch Kay so I could rest.

It was the longest week.

The day before the next ultrasound, I went to the bathroom. Held my breath as I had been, and sat down. One slight push to relieve myself and something dropped out of me. When I stood to look, I couldn't make sense of what it was. A clot? Was that possible? But it seemed harder. Resting at the bottom of the bowl, it looked more like a cocoon or a pinecone. I flushed the toilet and hoped, whatever it was that left my body didn't have my baby inside it.

Finally, the day of the ultrasound came, and I held on to hope, even while knowing bleeding for a week wasn't anything to be positive about. I couldn't speak on the car ride there. My head stayed up against the head rest, my eyes closed, in silent prayer.

I was restless in the waiting room chair, surrounded mostly by expectant mothers with swelling bellies and broad smiles on their face. The palms of their hands made soft, wide circles on their mounds. *Don't cry, you'll scare them,* I said to myself. I was relieved to be called in and have the privacy of a room, my distress no longer exposed.

The OBGYN, a name and face I was not familiar with, and not a part of the midwife team I was used to, came in. She was cold. She made terrible eye contact. She was medical. There was no feeling in anything she said or did. Her words when the wand was inside me, showing my womb on the screen: "There's nothing there."

I couldn't make out whatever followed. It was the second time I had produced sounds I didn't recognize as my own. My nails dug into the sheet. My breastbone actually felt like it might snap in two.

At some point, she left and then came back. She shoved information about miscarriages in front of us, and told us we could go out the back way. Whether that was to offer us privacy, or protect the waiting room from our pain, I don't know. All I know was I had a healthy baby over a week ago, and now I had no baby. And there wasn't anything I could do to stop it or to change it.

The days that followed felt cryptic. How was I supposed to lay to rest a life that was never physically held? A body never formed? Yet a heartbeat I heard. A picture I saw. A life that grew inside me. A love that was born the moment the test read *positive*. How was I going to honor that I had two children, even if only one existed in *this* world? Navigating how to memorialize and honor what did not physically exist was new. Raw. Overwhelming.

What I could lean into was what I had learned from all the losses before then. That time would eventually ease some of the suffering. Even though I had no control of my body, it wasn't my fault. That some things are unexplainable, and accepting them is actually less painful than holding on to theories of *why*. That not being silent, not shrouding my feelings, that giving it a name, was healing.

So that's where I began. I began by calling closest family and friends and telling them I was pregnant and had miscarried. I began by writing a letter to my baby about being their mother. I began by forgiving my body. I began by forgiving You and God, and gave over trust You needed them for something more than I did. And I began by giving my baby a name.

I maneuvered the initial pain, grief, and loss using the lessons You already provided me. I came through to the other side, eventually having more good days than bad ones. But there's not a moment when I see a new baby, or buy a baby gift for a friend, that I don't think of the one I lost. There's not a January or early February when I don't remember that eighth week leading into the ninth. Or an August when I don't think about how old they would be now, and what personality they might have had, or how close they would have been with Kay. Or the adventures the three of us would have gone on.

Where I find my greatest solace is in thinking my baby is held in the arms of the people who have gone before me. And because that's a fine group of people, I know my baby is in loving and capable hands until I get there. It doesn't take the ache away, but it softens it. So, let those angels of mine up There know I'm counting on them, and tell my blessed little one their mama loves them.

With ache and longing,

B's mama

QUESTIONS FOR YOUR PATH TO BRAVERY

How have you braved a loss?

How has one loss helped you navigate another?

Letter 19
HOUSE MADE OF STRAW

Dear Big and Divine Bad Wolf,

Sometimes I think of 2017 as a tornado. A sneaky one. One no one saw coming, so there was no escape plan. No extra cans of food in storage, no flashlights ready. No generators. The storm came quickly, spun up dirt and dust, and blew the house down.

I never could have predicted my marriage would fall apart, I would miscarry my second child, move back in with my parents, sell our first house, file for divorce, and I would suddenly be organizing 50-50 custody schedules and grappling with the idea of being with Kay only half the time.

The life I once saw as completely solid had actually been made of straw. A couple key gusts of wind, and it all collapsed.

It was like one day we were all standing upright.

The next day, I couldn't believe my eyes. The house was flattened.

I blame myself. For not being honest with myself. Then not with my husband. And then once I *was* honest, there was no turning back. I couldn't undo it—what I said or didn't say. What I did or didn't do. The way I felt, or what I now recognized.

It was a confusing and difficult time. But if I had learned nothing else, what I knew was to trust You. Trust You had a reason. A plan. Trust this was all for the better, even though it felt like a giant sinkhole had opened beneath me.

I started spending a lot of time looking backward. Retracing my steps. Figuring out my errors. Trying to make sense of the mess that was now my life.

One night I sat on my bed at my parent's house—Kay was with his dad—and I started going through a folder my parents had found and left on the bedspread. Inside was a copy of my high school graduation speech, which I had given as class president. Copies of glowing recommendation letters written by all my internship supervisors for my graduate school application. Other certificates and awards of achievement were tucked inside. My acceptance letter to the Psy.D program I turned down.

I spread these mementos out and looked at them. This was evidence, at one point, I believed I could, and I was determined to be someone *important*. Someone with a great title, who made contributions to the career she chose. Someone who was also a family woman. A woman to watch, excelling in all areas. I had been a young woman with direction, and motivation. Fire.

When did I last feel like that? I wondered. Or what did it even mean anymore?

I thought about how I had gone after my M.F.A. About what I had achieved in teaching women's studies. The passion I had for advocacy, women's rights, women's empowerment, and I recognized the last time I had truly engaged with any of that part of myself was in grad school—seven years removed, at that point.

I had known what I was doing once. I had a good plan. I had a grasp on what a happy and successful life was supposed to look like. Or I thought I did.

Really, I had performed all the roles that looked right, felt right, and I'd subscribed to everyone else's ideas, wants, and wishes, and had tried to claim them as my own. To squeeze myself into someone else's box. Perhaps my old Accomplishment-Identity had finally proved it wasn't healthy—checking off all the boxes under the category of *Successful Life* would never give me what I was really after.

I leaned back against the wall. My chest ached. My head hurt. I couldn't remember the last time I had a good night's sleep—one where my thoughts didn't roll over themselves, tumbling around and tangling. I wondered if Kay was lost without me, feeling like less of a mother not being with him. Which only made my chest ache more. He wasn't even two yet.

As much as I loved my little boy, I recognized I had become complacent in this wife-and-mother role. Looking after the household. Looking after their needs. The needs of our extended families. Thinking I had all I wanted. Thinking I had made it. I had what any woman could ask for. I should be appreciative. Grateful. Have no complaints.

But where was *I* in all of that? Or was it wrong to want more for myself?

I had the 'happily ever after' I had dreamt about since a little girl. Didn't I? It looked like it from the outside, didn't it? I had the husband, the house with the fence, the dog, the cat, and just nearly two children. This was the picture-perfect model, right? So, what was the problem? How did my life end up here—on the path to divorce, living again in my parent's house, working at another unfulfilling job?

It was because I never quite figured out how to stand in my own power, right? (Is that You nodding?) Is that what all of this is about? To stay solid and true to myself. To seek no one else's permission. No one else's validation. To follow *my* own path, live my life by my rules, and have strength in who I am?

To determine my own picture of what's happy and successful. Sure, I get that *now*. I wish I had figured it out so much sooner.

In every relationship—not just marriage, and not even just in romantic relationships—I compromised myself. I didn't confront what bothered me for fear of hurting others' feelings, or because doing so never got me anywhere. I didn't pursue interests, because other people didn't understand why they were important to me.

I didn't speak or laugh loudly if the people with me hated to be the center of attention, which my presence naturally drew. I reserved pointing out anyone else's faults, or how their behavior contributed to the challenges they were facing, because they couldn't hear it.

I showed interest in their interests, so they would feel seen and interesting, but I never demanded or requested it in return. Whatever it was I needed, I didn't say. Sometimes, because I didn't know. Other times, because I wanted to avoid arguments. And most of the time, because I wanted them to know me so well I didn't have to say anything at all.

I know now, it doesn't work like that.

In all my *not doing,* in all my silence, in all my complacency, and in all my people-pleasing, I have contributed to a great many of my relationships not working. My marriage included (and especially). I can see that now.

Ultimately, if I had loved myself enough...had seen myself enough. Understood my own worth. Claimed my own space. Identified my own needs. Validated my own interests and desires. Given myself permission to go after what mattered to me. Been strong enough to be authentic and wave a middle finger at anyone who wanted to keep me small or in a box…I would have responded differently to family, friends, and partners. Or chosen different ones to begin with.

I would have had healthier relationships along the way. All because the one I had with myself would have been powerful.

You did your best to show me this the whole time. There were plenty of places on the path where You were trying to teach me all this. I just never saw what You wanted me to see. Instead, it took You making me a mom to realize what I wanted for myself, and then blowing down my house for me to finally stop, take a breath, and see.

It sucked. It was hard. It wasn't pretty.

But it set me free.

This time, there was no doubt: You (and the J-man himself) were carrying me.

In You I trust,

The failed wife, imperfect mother, and slow-to-love-herself enough human You've been carrying this whole time

QUESTIONS FOR YOUR PATH TO BRAVERY

What does it mean to you to love and accept yourself in ways that allow you to live the life you dream?

What can you do today to love yourself more?

What do you need to be honest with yourself about? How will that truth set you free?

Letter 20
TWINKLE, TWINKLE LiTTLE STAR

Dear Instructor of the Dance Called Life,

When the shit was swirling, and I was trying to put the pieces of my life back together, I decided it was time I finally work self-care into my routine. With my parents support, I was able to move into a condo closer to work, and a gym was around the corner. I decided to fold Zumba into my schedule on the days I didn't have Kay.

I had tried Zumba back when I first returned home from grad school, as a friend was obsessed with it and thought I would enjoy it. Always up for trying something new, I went with her to a class. She wanted to be up at the front of the room. Having no idea what I was about to get myself into, I followed. Had I been alone, I would have positioned myself in the back for the first couple of sessions, to see what this was all about.

I didn't know the routines everyone else did. I didn't know how to get my arms, legs, and hips all moving at the same time, but in different directions, or to a particular rhythm. I was frustrated with myself. And embarrassed. I worried about what the instructor thought, and if I was messing her up—and everyone else around me—by *not doing it right.*

So, the next time I went to a class, I chose the back. And again. And again. Eventually I stopped going altogether, because I moved, and changed jobs, and my schedule changed…

But that was *then*.

Zumba now felt different, in this weirdly dark time in my life. As soon as I walked in to my first class, the instructor called me out, seeing my unfamiliar face in her crowd of loyal Tuesday class members.

"Hey, newbie! Is this your first introduction to Zumba?"

"No. But my first time in awhile," I told her, and put my water bottle down along the wall. The room was packed.

"Hey, everyone! We got a newbie in our class. Say 'HI NEWBIE!'"

Everyone shouted in unison, "HI NEWBIE!"

I laughed, waved, and apologized in advance to the stranger to my right, in case I ended up throwing off their groove.

Class was a full hour. I messed up, move after move after move. I didn't know the routines. I didn't know the steps. I moved left while everyone else moved right.

Suddenly, what came flooding into me was the "Twinkle, Twinkle Little Star" routine I had messed up in a dance recital when I was four years old.

My parents signed my sister up for dance class. My sister was good at dance. She enjoyed the tutus and the costumes. She was excellent at following the teacher's instructions and memorizing the steps. Not to mention actually *doing* the steps.

Me? Not so much.

I hated tights, sequins, and scratchy tulle. Which seemed to be standard in dance costumes. I also didn't listen (apparently), and I was not so hot about following, memorizing, or doing the steps. The instructor asked my mother if I had A.D.D., as I was always distracted and doing my own moves in the back of the room. When the time came for our dance recital, we did a routine to "Twinkle, Twinkle Little Star." Except there was nothing routine about what I was doing in my row. As my mother tells it, I was so embarrassed and frustrated, I quit dance altogether.

For so long, I thought that whole experience was about the fact my sister was good at dance, and I wasn't. That my sister could listen and following along, and I couldn't. That she was liked and valued by the instructor for both of those qualities, and I wasn't. Of course, now I recognize that's not what it was about.

It was about being bold enough to be different. To find my own rhythm, because I liked it better the way I did it. To create something new (different steps) out of something I was given (routine steps). The instructor asked my mother if I had A.D.D. because she didn't know what to do with me. My energy. My desire to go my own way, instead of hers. I wasn't meant for dancing someone else's dance.

I get it now.

So there in Zumba, while we shimmied and shook, and (at times) dry humped the air, I didn't give two fucks I wasn't getting it down perfectly. I was going left when they went right. My body roll wasn't as rhythmic and sensual as the instructor's. (I mean, I had rolls, but they didn't know *how to* roll, if You catch my drift.) My feet didn't perfectly match the steps, the ones everyone else around me already knew by heart.

None of that mattered. I didn't go there to be perfect. Or to be a dancer. Or to learn a routine. I went because I wanted to do something for myself.

I did it imperfectly.

I did it boldly.

I did it my way.

Finally starting to get it,

Your little star

QUESTIONS FOR YOUR PATH TO BRAVERY

If being perfect were illegal, what would you finally give yourself grace to do imperfectly?

What rules or routines do you follow that don't serve you and why? How can you release them or replace them?

Letter 21
ANNE WiTH AN 'E'

Dear Universe,

Those early weeks in the condo trying to navigate the "new normal" were extremely quiet and lonesome on the days and nights without Kay. The time was good for self-reflection and exploration, but it was also hard to be trapped in my own mind, unfolding layers of my life, trying to sort and iron them out.

I found myself watching movies that reminded me of childhood and brought me comfort. It was an easy way to distract my mind from falling too deeply into a pit and feeling like it may not have the strength to climb back out. I was worried I might get stuck down there.

One of my childhood favorites had been *Anne of Green Gables*, a made for TV mini-series from 1985, starring Megan Follows as Anne, and Jonathan Crombie as Gilbert. (Who didn't have the hots for Gilbert Blythe?) It's about a wildly imaginative orphaned girl (Anne) who wins over the hearts of her adoptive family (Marilla and Matthew) and the people of the town called Avonlea. My mother was the one who introduced me to this series, having read the books herself as a child. I imagined she loved it because, 1. her name was Anne (complete with an 'E'); 2. it was set in the late 19th century, and my mom was always kind of a history buff; and 3. because my mom was a book worm (just like the protagonist, Anne).

My mom was often found in her recliner reading a book. While her reading tastes have changed dramatically over the years, she remains a reader. Someone who'd much rather get lost at home, in the pages of a book, than in any gathering of people.

I love the memories I have of watching *Anne of Green Gables* with my mom. That we could quote the next line. Laugh at the same joke. Cry at the same plot point. Cheer at the same victory. And most importantly, be enamored with Gilbert (Anne's childhood nemesis turned love interest). We always watched it in the fall. As the weather got cooler and the temperature outside in the woods grew less conducive to singing and dancing barefoot. There would be snuggly blankets, and cups of hot cocoa, and freshly baked muffins.

I loved the characters of Green Gables and Avonlea so much I desperately wanted them to be a part of my life. And I loved Anne. I wanted my own real-life Anne Shirley as a bosom buddy.

I loved Anne because I felt like I understood her. Anne talked to herself in a mirror. I talked to trees. Anne had a violent temper. I had a sharp and fast tongue. Anne had a wild imagination and a flare for the dramatic. I did, too. The one difference between us was I wasn't orphaned, though I did often feel misplaced. As a child, I watched Anne and saw a friend. A kindred spirit. A fellow black sheep. I saw Anne's story as one about finding a home and a family—simply put, and understated.

But there, as an adult, lying on my couch, missing Kay, I saw Anne as a child who grew into an adult and struggled between choosing herself and forging her own path, or choosing to belong.

I saw a woman struggling to break through the circumstances she was handed. Or tear through the boxes people tried to push her in. I saw a person who learned all she was after was inside her the whole time. I saw her finally stand in her own authentic power and grace. I saw a woman who recognized love wasn't a fairytale, and it didn't look the way it looked in books.

I watched *Anne of Green Gables* and recognized my journey and Anne's were the same. This fictional character really was my kindred spirit.

I recognized in my own life, how long I'd spent so desperately wanting to belong, be loved, and be accepted. How I had often stifled, internalized, or silenced some of the very qualities, gifts, and talents that made me magnificent. And I have suffered for it.

I also saw I hadn't been alone, even if, at times, I felt misunderstood. While I could see how my mom may have enjoyed Anne, I could see how my mom may have also related to Marilla (Anne's adoptive mother). Marilla wanted to curb and channel Anne's wild imagination, her temper, her flare for the dramatic, for Anne's own good, while also loving every bit of her for those very qualities. Marilla had once been sharp-tongued and quick to temper herself. Marilla had once had her own hopes and dreams, but chose duty and responsibility, which kept her at Green Gables, her parents' home.

I looked back and saw my mom as my first editor, correcting my grammar and spelling. Helping me hole punch my pages and put them into folders. She made beautiful clothes for my favorite doll. She once made a man for me out of cardboard (a refrigerator box) in the likeness of Danny Zuko, when I was obsessed with the movie musical *Grease*. She sewed me costumes and dress up clothes. She helped me practice my lines for school plays. When the great debate over where I was going to college got heated between me and my dad, she advocated for me, knowing how much my heart wanted to be there. She flew to Ohio on more occasions than I could count. She stood with me at the V-Day fundraiser that second year.

My mom had been my champion the entire time. Which meant if my mom had been cheering me on this entire time, and I had failed to see it clearly, who else had been in my corner?

Perhaps I had been living in my own Avonlea and failed to see it. There was that mix of both small-minded people I couldn't claim, *and* those who had been rooting for me from the beginning. Who were just waiting to see me take off for the moon, so they could say proudly, "We knew she was going places." People who wanted to see me succeed. People who wanted to see me accomplish my dreams. People who were ready to celebrate with me.

I watched that movie and I saw me. My journey. My mother, family, community. It all started to make sense. I started to see the path I had been on differently. Started to understand myself more clearly.

Hopefully yours,

Founding member of the Anne (with an E)
Bosom Friends Club

QUESTIONS FOR YOUR PATH TO BRAVERY

What parts of your journey can be reinterpreted now that you've had time and distance?

What parts of where you've been, directly impact where you're going?

Letter 22
BE BRAVE, BE YOU—ACT THREE

Dear Supreme Know-it-All,

While self-care like Zumba and watching nostalgic movies may have been comforting after my house was blown down, they weren't the answers to my most pressing concerns.

I had immediate questions like: Would I be okay financially as a single earner? How would I manage motherhood, now that my time as a parent had been halved? How would we work the holidays? Would Kay struggle? Which friends would I lose? What would people think of me? How do I parent solo effectively and consistently? How do I remain sane? What will I tell Kay when he's older?

Then there were much larger philosophical questions, too: Who was I? Who did I want to be? What did I want from life? As a person. As a mom. As a professional. How would I ever forgive myself for deconstructing the family I created? My contribution to the failure of my marriage, and my guilt and shame that came with it, were very real. And it was heavy.

The only way to sort through the enormous amounts of emotional cataloging was to begin journaling again. (And keep going to therapy, of course. God bless Celia!) Somewhere along the way, I had stopped. I couldn't even recall when. Probably around the time I thought I had

164

found my happily ever after. Around the time when life felt safe and steady, and so there was 'no need' to write and release and express and explore.

Yes, another example of failing to show up for myself. I hear You. (You are such a know-it-all... yes, I know that's actually true.)

Through journaling. I began to process.

Through journaling, I woke that sleeping young girl who always loved words. A victory! Some part of me was still left. The part of me that always felt strength when her hands touched a pen or a keyboard. That part of me still lived.

As the weeks turned into months and I navigated separation and shared custody, I started to embrace the silver linings of parenting only half the time. It was the only perspective possible, otherwise the weight of missing Kay, and feeling like a terrible mother, would have broken me.

The days that weren't scheduled days to have Kay allowed me to chip away at the list of legal to-dos, to go to therapy, to get some exercise, to engage in self-care, and to re-find myself.

What came back the swiftest were my writing dreams. Writing had been so loyal a companion—always there when I needed it, even after long dry spells. A true and everlasting love. I was tired of ignoring it. Tired of waiting for anyone to tell me I had permission to pursue it. And now, there was nothing to stop me, but me.

I had thought for years about an author website, a way to start establishing my writer's platform, but had never taken any action. For years, I had wanted to establish a writing practice but hadn't done so. For years I had been thinking about picking my grad thesis back up. For years, I had started new manuscripts and then walked away from them nearly as soon as they began.

Excuses. Lack of confidence. Choosing other activities. Picking people and social gatherings instead of writing, etc.

No more.

I had promised myself as a little girl I would be a writer. I promised myself as a mom, I would model for my son that he could pursue his dreams.

What was I waiting for?

Sitting in the margins of my own story had produced no results. Doing all the other stuff—the 'right things,' the 'normal things'—hadn't gotten me where I wanted to be. It was time to leap into the middle of the page and quit operating on the sides of my passion or trying to fit between other people's lines.

With the talents and support of a colleague, my author website went up. I had headshots taken. I produced business cards. I started a blog. Began growing an email list. I got onto Instagram and started a Facebook business page. People were writing to me or leaving comments on my posts—people shared with me parts of their own stories they had never uttered, responding to words I had written and shared.

My whole platform became: Be Brave. Be You. It's Time.

Parts of my soul found their way back to each other. As though they had been separated and were trying to find each other again all this time. I began to re-believe I wasn't such a horrible human being after all.

A writing friend, Mara, offered a free week-long course to work on a book project. I dragged out that old thesis, and I committed to the one-week. Miraculously, I discovered my writing voice. This was *epic*. The one piece of consistent feedback from my thesis committee way back then was that my voice was not present on the page.

Now, years later, one free writing course, and there it was. I felt it. I knew it. And it was exhilarating. I made Mara my writing coach.

The more I engaged with my writing side, the truer I felt. My spirit lifted. My emotional energy shifted. I felt stronger and braver. I felt more real. I was doing right by myself and Kay. There was redemption.

I would no longer fail me. Or him. I would make something out of this passion. Just as I had told my dad on the phone, when I called him to let him know I was switching Master's. I was recharged, with a force that would not be reckoned with. I didn't know where it would lead, but I could feel it. Tides were changing.

Then, there was a call posted online from a local mom's blog looking for writers. I had seen this same post several months prior, but the timing wasn't right. But, right then? I was willing to take a chance. I was ready.

I applied. I was asked to interview. I was accepted. I started writing for them immediately. My blog posts generally performed well, and the comments I received were positive and accepting. People seemed to like what I had to say. How I said it. My words were resonating with readers. Not just the friends and family I had called to my personal blog, but with complete strangers reading about my 'mom experiences' via someone else's blog.

The more I wrote, the more I wanted to write. The more I dreamt about writing. The more I thought about how I could make this more monetarily valuable. The more I daydreamed at work, and the more I jotted down new ideas or thought about what to do next with my platform.

The job I went to after the law firm, the one with promises of promotion and advancement, no longer fueled me as it had. I needed the paycheck and the benefits to support myself and Kay, but it wasn't my final resting place. The admin role I didn't climb out of wasn't what I was meant to do. I could feel that again, so strongly.

You must have heard me, then. My own internal whispers. You must have felt my inner flame burning brightly.

Any remaining hope of advancement at that day job crumbled. The last part of my previous life tossed on top of the rubble. I was brought into a scheduled meeting and told I was not getting the promotion I was promised. The company would hire externally for that position. Additionally, some of my current responsibilities were being stripped from my duties. I was essentially demoted, even though I was already at the lowest rung on the ladder. Any lower and I would have been terminated altogether.

I still have no idea what all of that was about, but clearly, the end of that employment was coming. I didn't know which one of us would call it quits first—me or them—but I knew my time there was limited.

Since I desperately did not want to be fired, for a multitude of obvious reasons, I started to look at jobs and consider yet another employment change. Begrudgingly, I started looking at help-wanted ads. Updating my resume. Redrafting my cover letter. I hated the whole process.

When I found a position at a local university in the women's center, my whole heart filled. How fond I had been of working in the women's studies department, and with college students.

This was it! Yes! It must be!

Nope.

I interviewed, and it went well, but ultimately, they suspended the search.

Instead of feeling devastated—which I had expected—I felt relief. I felt You again, guiding me. *That wasn't the answer*, I heard You saying.

I suspended my own search. I would not go after another traditional job until I understood more about what I was looking for.

I surrendered.

"What are You trying to tell me?" I asked You. "I'm trusting in You. You always seem to get me to the other side. So, I'm leaving it to You."

(I wish I could have seen Your face in that moment…assuming You *have* a face…)

In surrendering, You presented *the* window.

Working with Mara one afternoon on a book project, I gave her the rundown on my miserable 9–5 life. She told me about becoming a virtual assistant.

"What's that?" I asked.

She described it as someone working from home who performs admin responsibilities for business owners. While the admin part sounded dreadful—as I had already been stuck in that loop long enough already—the working from home, setting my own hours, sounded worthy of pursuit.

"You don't have to just focus on admin stuff," Mara told me, as she saw my nose curl.

She pointed me to the exact woman to speak to: Cat. Cat then invited me to take her five-day challenge. In the five-day challenge, she talked about various tracks you could focus on in your business. Among them was writing.

I could work from home, write, and get paid?

What?!

EUREKA!

I finally figured out how to make my passion my living.

I finally would make my dream of being a writer come true.

Stars aligned. Heavens parted. Lightning struck. (You know, the whole shebang.)

I had a breakthrough call with Cat when the challenge was over, and I knew it was EXACTLY where You wanted me.

I enrolled in Cat's Expert VA Training program. *Domino down.*

A month later, I formed my business. *Domino down.*

A month after that, I had paying clients. *Domino down.*

And three and a half months later—I had saved enough money to walk away from my day job. *Domino down.*

Leaning into the passion that had always been there and leveraging a gift I had been given, I was reinvented, which brought new vitality—in the way I parented, in the way I connected with others, in the way I took care of and saw myself.

The strengths and resilience I felt when I was first introduced to women's studies returned. The ghost of my childhood self, who danced barefoot in the trees with abandon, flickered in the corner of my eye.

Some kind of homecoming happened, and it was because I chose to be brave. I chose to uncover a part of me that had long been pushed under. I chose to listen (finally) to what You, oh dazzling Universe, had been trying to tell me this *whole* time.

I was choosing to remember what I once knew through to my core—I was born to be a writer.

In celebration that I finally made it,

An emerging writer and entrepreneur

QUESTIONS FOR YOUR PATH TO BRAVERY

What are your Truths that you know about yourself deep inside?

Which do you want to explore or cultivate?

Afterword
HOW *DEAR UNIVERSE* CAME TO BE

A week after I walked out of my day job, I flew to Missouri to attend Kathy's (known as Cat in the prior chapter) live event for all those in her program. It was a three-day conference for creating successful, virtual-based businesses from our homes. I couldn't wait to meet people I had spent the last six months cultivating relationships with online. I couldn't wait to celebrate with Kathy and my coach, Mary, that I had walked out of my day job only days before. Both thanks to their support and mentorship.

On the first full day, a speaker, Debbie, with short bright pink hair and glitter eyeshadow, stepped to the front of the room. She identified herself as a seer and empath, an intuitive. I had no idea what any of that meant at the time. But as soon as she started to speak, I leaned in. Debbie commanded the room with intensity and light, and her personal story was gripping. I hung on her every word. She told us about being robbed at gunpoint, and about her dark descent into depression and PTSD.

She moved me to tears. I know that feeling of being robbed of your safety, your control, your sense of security, though in my experience, the weapon was of flesh and not of steel. I also know the struggle to overcome it. I was drawn to her bravery. Her vulnerability. I was moved by her strength. I was in awe of how this harrowing tale has become a part of her platform and brand. And in that moment listening to her, *I knew instantly* what I wanted to do with my business.

I wanted to ghostwrite and publish women's stories of adversity, grit, hope, and triumph. I needed to connect with other women like Debbie, this pink haired *wondress* (a self-made word I've given her—the combination of *goddess* and *wonder*). I would write for women who were successful in their businesses and industries while also having overcome immense challenge, trauma, adversity.

I needed to hear these stories, and then I needed to tell them. I needed to write them or help them be written. These stories must be told. The world must have them. The world must hear them. The world must be changed.

But how?

I left that event knowing the direction I wanted to go, but I didn't know where to start.

Until, in the early morning hours a few weeks later, I had a vision that came to me as I was coming out of sleep. A book with a black and white composition cover. *Dear Universe* as the title. That was it.

I started to think about the future ideal client who may want to work with me to write their book, and it occurred to me they might ask if I had published words of my own. Had I braved my own path to put myself out there? To tell my own stories. To be vulnerable. To be seen and heard. To offer my own stories to the world. I would have to say 'no,' unless…

Dear Universe became the answer.

This book would become the marketing activity and social validation, to prove to my future ideal client what I could help them achieve. But what exactly would it focus on? What exactly would I say? I found myself starting to doubt I had anything to say at all. Limiting beliefs crept in, and I stalled on writing.

The visions of the book persisted. The idea kept moving around inside me. Little chunks of text and content were floating in and out. Occasionally, I jotted them down in a nearby notebook. I kept my mind open to what I needed to receive. Waiting to be guided. (You know, by the Universe, of course).

And then, the missing piece came in loud and clear.

I went to a networking luncheon for a new local chapter focused on women in business. I heard this amazing speaker—the woman who had created the foundation—and she talked about the lessons we learn along our journeys. That the Universe provides what we need—the right lessons and experiences.

She said, "The Universe is doing it *for you*, not to you."

From there, she went on to say the Universe gives you shit to deal with when the stakes are low, because later, when the stakes are higher, you might get a similar whiff of that same event or emotion or lesson again. Except this time, you'll know what to do. You'll recognize it. And you can either forget everything you learned the last time and run, or remember everything from before and rise.

That was it: letters to the Universe on the journey, and lessons along the way.

The subtitle, *I Get it Now,* came to mind.

While the direction for content now seemed clear, I still didn't know how to drill it down to the individual letters or themes that were relevant to me. So, I let the idea marinate some more.

Around this time, I was working with a local branding strategist, Julia. She asked me to fill out this very intense and detailed questionnaire. There were questions about me personally, questions about my business and visions, and questions about my prior educational and work experiences. In reading my answers and interviewing me, she was able to zero-in immediately on how my education, my experiences, my long and winding personal journey, made me exactly the right person to offer my writing services and work with my ideal client.

In having formal writing education, I knew how to craft a good story.

In having experience working in mental health, I understood how to listen and communicate with people. To see them, hear them.

In having various work experiences, I had a ridiculous amount of skills to leverage that would make me a successful business owner, but also someone who could deliver exceptional customer service and project management.

In having had bad shit happen sometimes, I could approach clients with empathy, compassion, understanding, and humor.

When she handed this summation to me in the form of my brand summary, it hit me hard and fast. These experiences, attributes, skills, gifts wove together. Suddenly I was looking back on my journey and understanding how it all lined up. How it all worked together to bring me to this moment. How these elements of my experience and my personality uniquely position me as a professional writer. But also, how all these make me uniquely me.

The specific lessons and letters of this book started to form in my mind.

There it was—the vision of the cover, the title and subtitle, the focus, and even some of the letters and yet, I avoided writing this book for months.

Despite all the work I had done to step into my power, to recognize my strengths, and to be brave in life and in business, I could not put my butt in the chair. I resorted to old habits of not making time and space for my creative work. Of choosing other activities. Of course,

I was running a business and being a mom, so it wasn't like I wasn't choosing high priorities. But I *did believe* in this book, so why was I holding back? What was blocking me?

The answer was me. Which I knew. But why? Hadn't I already worked out that I needed to pursue my own passions? That no one was going to do this for me?

I needed to figure this out, or I was going to keep on doing this. And I had so many other books in my heart.

I turned to the pink-haired *wondress* to learn about soul essences and auras. Debbie told me I was an essence of creation. As an essence of creation, I'm naturally tethered to the idea of perfectionism, to my writing needing to be meaningful, and to the sense of belonging. In being a perfectionist, I couldn't get past starting something, because I feared once it was finished, it wouldn't be perfect. And if it wasn't perfect, I couldn't put it out there for anyone. In needing what I wrote to be meaningful, or to create an experience for others that was meaningful, I needed to ensure what I said was meaningful, and they would find meaning in it…

But what if what I had to say didn't matter to them? And in not mattering, I was not accepted, and in not being accepted, I didn't feel like I belonged? And in not feeling like I belonged, there was no point in having written anything to begin with…

I needed to get this under control. I needed to flip all these scripts.

I flew to Utah.

Debbie was holding a live event where she took people on a deep exploration of their essences and helped them to understand how to bring their creative work to light by understanding themselves more. By leaning into their gifts and strengths, while watching out for slips into 'shadow' (or being out of alignment).

While I was there, this was what I learned:

Each of us matters. I matter. You matter. If I matter, then what I have to say matters. So, I can write what is in my heart, because it matters. And it's going to matter to at least one other person. And if it matters to at least one other person, then there is meaning; and if there is meaning, there is connection; and with connection, belonging.

While I was there, I started to create a framework to keep myself focused on these ideas.

I flew back home.

I started writing.

I kept writing.

Along the way, I have committed myself to these ideas:

This book is meant to be powerful not perfect.

This book is brave, and it belongs in this world.

This book fulfills the promise I made to myself a long time ago.

Now, here it is.

My first published work.

Now, it's no longer mine, but *ours*. I hope it matters to you. I hope it helps you. I hope it inspires you. I hope as a result of reading it, you're ready to look back on your own journey and figure out what it's offered you. What it's taught you. I hope in reading this, you're feeling brave to look back and look forward, but most importantly, to look in the mirror and *love* what you see.

Because it's time you be brave being you. You're a wonder. The Universe has made you so.

Letter 23
FINAL THANK YOU

Dear Universe,

I just wanted to thank you.

You gave me so many gifts.

I have this powerful voice that can be used as an agent of change, for creating connection and community, for advocacy, for inspiration…

I have this natural knack with people, to see them and hear them, to draw from them their stories, their light and darkness, and to hold space with them…

I have this way of wielding words, so I may capture truth, beauty, hope, love, determination, resiliency, tribulation on the page, and commit people's voices and messages to memory.

You have given me all I need to make for myself a life I can be proud of, a life full of meaning, wonder, adventure, connection, and love. A life of my own design.

You have given me the strength to keep going, to be brave, and to model for my son what it means to listen to your heart and stand in your own power.

You have led me everywhere I've needed to be, and you have

brought me here.

I get that now.

With love and gratitude,

A.Y., professional writer

Bravery Boosters
MORE STUFF FOR THE READER

I want to be clear about something. Bravery looks different to each of us. We are going to define it differently, as we apply our own personal experience and lens to what we consider being brave. And we are all going to have different starting points. I may have been working on bravery for a long time, while others may just be beginning. I may be super brave in one area of my life and terrible in another.

Bravery can also shift, based on the context. Bravery in the face of adversity, versus bravery in facing an old story/narrative, versus bravery in standing up for one's self won't all exhibit the same way. It may also change, moment to moment. Everything is always evolving. Especially people. (Or so I hope. How depressing would it be if we all remained exactly the same, day after day?)

The bravery you're trying to cultivate for yourself and your life is yours to define. As such, the suggestions here are open-ended and broad, to allow you to breath your own purpose into them.

ANSWERING THE QUESTIONS INSIDE THIS BOOK

Not everyone wants to journal and reflect through writing. You probably thought all those questions I asked you throughout this book were meant for you to noodle around and then jot down on paper. The thing is, I know not everyone reflects or sorts through information in the same way. I may have an affinity for keeping a journal and processing through the written word, but that does not mean you do.

If journaling is *your jam*, then awesome. Grab a designated notebook and go. If it's not, consider the questions as ones you can reflect on while:

- meditating
- going for a walk (or doing any form of exercise)
- taking a drive
- knitting or crocheting (or something where your hands are busy, but your mind is free)
- speaking with a trusted confidant (or a therapist)

You can also use these questions as prompts for other creative outlets. For instance, try painting or collaging your reflection to the question. Writing a piece of music—instrumental or with words—that expresses the answer to the question. Taking photographs that visually represent your reflections and answers.

There is no wrong way to find the answers to the questions posed in this book.

5 BRAVERY BOOSTERS FOR BEGINNERS

Looking for more actions to improve your 'bravery muscles'? Here are some suggestions of low-cost options to give you a boost:

Read more books in the self-help/personal-development arena specific to an area in your life you want to develop.

Find a podcast that does a deep dive on a focused area of your life you are looking to cultivate.

Create a Pinterest board of all the things you would do if you were the bravest badass you knew, and then pick one thing from this board to work toward. (Think of this like a bucket list, except instead of it being about all the things you want to do before you die, it's all the things you want to do when you're brave enough to do them.)

Develop a power phrase or mantra (or find one you love—you know, on Google somewhere) and commit this to memory. Everyday say this phrase/mantra out loud to yourself several times. Set a reminder in your phone, if you need to, or plaster it around the house on a post-it note, and say it every time you see it. For example, you could try "I am enough and I have everything I need."

Make a wish list. What exactly is it you're wishing you or your life looked like by developing more bravery?

5 BRAVERY BOOSTERS FOR INTERMEDIATES

Here are some suggestions for going a little deeper:

Commit to one (self-defined) act of bravery each week. Ask a close friend to hold you accountable, so you don't chicken out.

Role play firing an old story or rule. Invite an old story or rule (that no longer serves you) to a meeting. Use your body, your voice, and your furniture to actually role play holding this meeting. Invite them in to sit. Let them know they're fired, but thank them for their service. Address what they've done to be helpful (this is where the thanks comes in) and then let them know why you're no longer in need of their service (this is the firing part.)

Sign up for an online challenge. There are tons of coaches and other service professionals who offer free challenges, where you get to develop new skills or explore new areas. Look at the Pinterest board you created or the wish list you made, and go find an online challenge that may help you actualize one of the items you captured.

Write and burn your grudges and regrets. Are you carrying around old weight of the people who did wrong against you? Or regrets in life from missing an opportunity or failing to respond in a particular way to something? Time to let it go. Jot these grudges and regrets down and then burn them (yes, incinerate them), and finally let that shit go.

Create your own rule book. Identify what rules (or values) you want to live by. However you want to keep that information (list, pictures, printed document), put it somewhere where you can access it readily. Review it regularly to check that you're living your life by your own design.

10 CHALLENGES TO ADVANCE YOUR BRAVERY

Want to go all in? Ready to really challenge yourself and the fear you might have of being judged, perceived, misunderstood, or unaccepted? Try these out:

Go to a restaurant and ask for a table for one. Yes, I mean eat alone. And when you ask for that table, try not to say "Just one." You're important and awesome. It's not 'just' you. It's you. You're fabulous.

See a movie by yourself. Order the biggest popcorn. Buy the biggest drink. Sit right in the middle of the theater. Don't hide away in the back corner.

Take a class on something totally new to you. Especially a class where you have a belief you 'suck at' that something.

Share an opinion or make a stance. If you're in a crowd (online or in person) with diverse thoughts and feelings on an issue, speak your mind anyway.

Plan and commit to specific *me-time.* No matter what the spouse/ partner says, or the kids need, or the to-do list shows. Make a plan for *me-time,* and commit to it. It could be an hour, it could be a whole weekend. The point is to design something tailored to you and your needs, wants, desires. and then execute.

Sing out loud with the windows rolled down. Or while you're running/exercising. If you're really brave, you can dance, too. (I double-dog dare you.)

Clear the air with old foes. Was there someone who really hurt you in the past? Or someone you hurt? Maybe it's time to clear the air and close the loop. Reach out to the people you've hurt and apologize. For those who hurt you, imagine they reach out to you. Issue a response. (You can do this in role play or in writing.)

Go to an event you're familiar with and introduce yourself to three new people. I bet even extroverts have a hard time with this. It's pretty easy to gravitate toward people we already know and to get so immersed in catching up with them we fail to extend ourselves to new faces. But the new faces are at a disadvantage. They've never been there before, and you have.

Go to an event you're NOT familiar with, and STILL introduce yourself to three new people. Prepare some conversation starters and practice them in the car before you arrive, so you don't have that initial "What do I say?" anxiety.

Roadtrip. By yourself. Yup. Pick a drive-able destination. Develop your travel itinerary. Pack your bag and go. Adventure awaits. See what you discover about yourself while you're away.

Acknowledgements

I know I dedicated this book to my parents, but truthfully, they have to be acknowledged again for, 1. giving me life, 2. accepting all the grey hairs I have given them along the way, and 3. tolerating their appearance in these pages.

I want to thank Douglas, my companion, sounding board, and biggest fan, who infused me with encouragement to keep going (sometimes via homemade chocolate chip cookies); listened attentively through the entire process of bringing this book to fruition (probably upwards of 100 hours); and read the very first (raw) draft and provided feedback (complete with funny notes in the margins and plenty to say about the Ninja Turtles chapter). Plus, he designed one hell of a web page for the book. So much love.

Thank you to the other members of my Council of BIG Famous—Adam, Sonia, Cindy, Paula—who either listened to this book via Voxer, or read the earliest drafts and provided their honest feedback. Your insight and suggestions were critical to the development of this work. A special shout out to Adam, who reminded me one day when the evil twins Doubt and Fear showed up to "Shush those bitches." To Cindy, who said to me, "You've already inspired all of us who got to read it first. You're on the right path. Keep going." To Sonia, for her everlasting friendship through the years and across the miles. You were a part of the other side of the world I am glad to have seen. Thank you for your critical, editorial eye, and for taking your holiday off to read the first draft in one-sitting.

An UTMOST SHOUT OUT OF THANKS to Paula (known as Mara within these pages). There are so many words. Thank you for helping me find my voice. Thank you for believing in me. Thank you for telling me about becoming a VA and pointing me in the right direction. Thank you for providing your assessment of this book. For all your professional direction, your friendship and support. A million freaking *thank yous* for all my days. I "heart you" so hard it hurts.

Thank you to my final wave of readers, Erica, Kameka, Shurice, Mikaela, and Heaven. The feedback you each provided in this final stage—from the little typos you caught, to the holes you still felt needed to be filled, to particular chapters you still felt needed reconsideration or tweaking, your suggestions felt like dressing this book up with a ribbon and bow and truly making it a gift I could give to the world.

Big, heart-filled thanks to Tammy and Debbie for reading and endorsing this work and seeing its heartbeat. With super extra thanks to Tammy for not just reading to endorse, but reading it with ferocious, laser-focused attention to development and detail. And *super-sized-extra-special-squishy-face-tackle-hugs* for Debbie, whose Claim Your Magic Intensive in the fall of 2019 gave me the tools, space, and self-understanding to create the original framework for this book.

Thank you to my book team: Moira, Chelsea, Lynelle, Angelic, Pat, Rachel (at Onion River Press), Jackie, Melissa, Susie, and Sarah. From publishing to promotion, you were one Rockstar team to have as I did this crazy thing of self-publishing a book. I'm so grateful for each one of your skills, talents, and expertise which brought this book to life.

For my friends and family who appeared in this work even if your names were changed, thank you for being a part of my journey and a part of these pages. Not in order of appearance: Jessica, Jameson, Meggan, Adam, Linda, Kameka, Cherie, Paula, Kathy, Krista, and Pat.

To all those I have named in this Acknowledgements section: I love you, I love you, I love you. I'm so very grateful for your presence on my journey and your part in making this dream come true.

Lastly, thank you to every single person who chooses to purchase and read this work. Remember: **Be brave. Be you. It's time.**

Fist Bumps for Females

Because it's especially important to me that women lift each other up and help each other rise, I've developed this special acknowledgements section for the badass women business owners/service providers who directly impacted the development, production, marketing, and publication of this book and cheer-leaded like hell from start to finish. I am so very grateful to each of them and blessed to have them in my corner.

Moira Abram-Hale, ridiculously awesome cover and interior designer | http://moiraabram.com

Jackie Barker, member of my book team who supported graphic design and communication activities for promotion and launch | https://barefootdigitalmarketing.com/

Debbie Burns, seer, empath, and pink-haired *wondress* within these pages, who endorsed this work | https://www.debbieburns.me/

Paula Diaco, my wise and beautiful writing coach and mentor, friend, and fellow writer | https://writestoriesnow.com/

Rachel Fisher, the publishing guru (and manager) at Onion River Press, who excelled in holding my hand during this process | https://www.phoenixbooks.biz/onionriverpress

Sarah Frey, my Fall of 2020 intern who dove right into the final stages of marketing and promotion | linkedin.com/in/sarah-frey152

Pat Goudey O'Brien, a supreme line editor, who turned this manuscript from scrappy to snappy | https://www.linkedin.com/in/pat-goudey-obrien-32546913/

Tammy Flanders Hetrick, friend, endorser, and fellow writer who encouraged me to add 10K additional words | http://www.tammyflandershetrick.com/

Abigail Lewis, my summer of 2020 intern, who created fabulous content for the book's landing page and helped to promote the book on my social media channels | https://www.linkedin.com/in/abigailgraylewis/

Lynelle Mykins, my Chief Operating Rockstar, who helped with a variety of promotional and launch items along the way | https://lmykinsva.com/

Chelsea Simmons, member of my book team, who took over my social media promotion and created beautiful downloadable content for my landing page | https://www.linkedin.com/in/chelsea-simmons-65519a35/

Susie Thomas, member of my book team who took on copywriting for the book's promotional and launch activities | https://solutionswriteaway.com/

Melissa Tradewell, member of my book team and newly-appointed author assistant | https://melissatradewellediting.com/

Angelic Veasman, dynamo proofreader and serious support of all virtual launch efforts | https://www.ladypowerhouse.com/

About the Author

A.Y. Berthiaume is a native Vermonter, professional writer, practicing feminist, recovering middle child, hobby junkie, wannabe superhero, and a mom who's pretty sure she's "winging it" most of the time, but hoping she makes it look good. She has an M.F.A. in creative writing from the NEOMFA Program. This is her first full-length, published work of ~~guts brilliance~~ creative nonfiction.

Berthiaume is the Lady Boss Owner (LBO) and bread*writer* at The Write Place, Right Time (TWPRT), a virtual boutique of copywriting and ghostwriting services. TWPRT works with women coaches, trainers, consultants, and speakers to craft emotionally compelling, authentic, and valuable content. She helps translate her client's expertise and experiences into accessible wisdom and advice for their audience. Through meaningful messaging and powerful stories that are told in the voice of her client, Berthiaume nurtures the connections between her clients and their tribe.

If you're looking for a sweet creative collaborator—that's spirited, compassionate, and *'hella'* fun to work with—to support you in word-wizarding your greatest stories into your greatest gifts, connect with her. Let her get your voice, your message, and your story onto the page…whenever you're ready.

WANT TO CONNECT?

Visit her at ayberthiaume.com to know more about her personal writing and thewriteplacerighttime.com to learn more about how she can 'do words' for you.

Sign up for both email lists. Become a stark raving fan.

WHAT YOU CAN DO IF YOU LIKE THIS BOOK

Review it on Goodreads and/or Amazon.

Tell all your friends about this book.

Buy all your friends this book.

Buy this book and give it to strangers.

Read it over and over and over again.

Beg for more.

CPSIA information can be obtained
at www.ICGtesting.com
Printed in the USA
FSHW020424071120
75636FS